Is God a Scientist?

Religious Views of Science

Daryl Culp

COPYRIGHT © 2016 by Daryl Culp

All rights reserved.

ISBN: 978-0-9953081-0-7
Ebook: 978-0-9953081-1-4

Table of Contents

Introduction 1
Methodological considerations 11
Religion and science: History 29
Biology: The God of life 53
Physics: Matter matters 77
Psychology and sociology: Psyche and spirit 107
Ecological considerations 141
Stories of salvation 153
Bibliography 177

Acknowledgements

I owe a profound debt of gratitude to the many teachers who have helped formulate my thoughts. Thanks also to my students who have helped clarify my thinking. I have taught a course on these topics at Lithuania Christian College, International University (Vienna), St. Michael's College (University of Toronto) and Humber College. Thanks to the Templeton Foundation for their grant supporting my first course on science and religion at Lithuania Christian College in 2001. Thanks to colleagues, friends and in-laws who have read drafts of sections of this manuscript and given helpful comments: Giosue Ghisalberti, Leo DiLeo, Paul Doerksen, Dennis Brooks, David Klassen, Katherine Anderson and Ken Reid. Thanks to Joyce Tan for help with cover design.

In the end, a belief in the existence of a final, ultimate spirit rests on a kind of faith. ... But also, everyone who is involved in the pursuit of science becomes convinced that some spirit is manifest in the laws of the universe.
Albert Einstein, answering a letter asking "Do scientists pray?"

Science! True daughter of Old Time thou art!
  Who alterest all things with thy peering eyes.
Why preyest thou thus upon the poet's heart,
  Vulture, whose wings are dull realities?
Edgar Allan Poe, "Sonnet—to science"

Sometimes it seems that scientific theories replace religious views of the world. Were human beings created by God or did we evolve from the other animals? Instead of seeing science and religion as opposites, many have tried to integrate the two perspectives (seeking to understand the "mind of God" that made the natural laws).[1] This book will survey attempts to relate science and religion. I will introduce the scientific ideas at an

---

[1] For a comprehensive overview of the issues in this field see Christopher Southgate *et al., God, Humanity and the Cosmos* (T & T Clark, 2005), which has summaries at: www.meta-library.net/ghc/index-frame.html. My website has additional research links: individual.utoronto.ca/darylculp/scixtn.html.

introductory level and pursue the theological issues in more depth.

Often discussions of this topic focus on the conflicts between religion and science. However, there are many ways to try to reconcile the two approaches. Some believers in the monotheistic religions try to accommodate the theory of evolution by interpreting the six days of creation as a metaphor indicating periods of time (as some say, "a thousand years is like a day in God's eyes"). Non-theistic religions may see the spiritual energy of the universe manifesting itself in the process of evolution. Michael Dowd says it this way: "'God' is the inner Love, or incomprehensible Life, at the heart of the process; the Great Mystery revealed in and through the Universe."[2] The universe itself can be seen as the creative spirit that develops the world which we experience.

Eastern religions have some fascinating ways to interpret the physical world as a manifestation of a deeper underlying spiritual reality. This way of religious thinking has less antagonism towards the dry technical understanding of the physical laws of nature. Instead, science can be seen as a first step for understanding the universe, but it must be completed by a deeper investigation. Hinduism speaks of the physical world as "maya," an illusion because it obscures a more fundamental spiritual reality.

In Hinduism, the god Brahma utters the primordial sound "OM" which brings forth the physical universe. The story, in summary, relates that "Brahma fashions a great world-egg, which contains the entirety of the phenomenal-empirical world."[3] In a more impersonal account, the *Rig Veda* says:

> THEN was not non-existent nor existent: there was no realm of air, no sky beyond it.

---

[2] Michael Dowd, "The Great Story." (http://thegreatstory.org/Bigpicture1.html)
[3] Gerald James Larson, "Hindu Cosmogony/Cosmology" in James W. Haag, Gregory Peterson and Michael Spezio, eds. *Routledge Companion to Religion and Science* (Routledge, 2012), 114.

> What covered in, and where? And what gave shelter?
> Was water there, unfathomed depth of water?
> Death was not then, nor was there aught immortal: no sign was there, the day's and night's divider.
> That One Thing, breathless, breathed by its own nature: apart from it was nothing whatsoever.
> (*Rig Veda* HYMN CXXIX)[4]

The verses above seem to indicate that all of the Hindu gods really stem from one primordial source (it is not named here but the Upanishads call it Brahman: note the slightly different spelling than the creator god). The word "Brahman" is used to refer to all of reality (especially the spiritual basis of that reality, even more than that which we see).

We might relate these ideas to concepts being explored today by scientists: "dark energy" and "dark matter." Both of these concepts are used to designate something that we don't yet understand (but that seem to be more fundamental than our current theories of energy and matter). It seems to me that religious metaphors also use this tangential strategy to get us to look beyond what seems obvious (because it has been accepted for so long). Religious metaphors seek to transcend the human sensory experience and indicate something more profound. Now, it may be that dark matter and energy will someday be explained by well-formed scientific theories. Religious metaphors could then shift the ground and encourage us to think beyond that explanation.

The idea of an invisible essence to the universe was expressed by Plato. He postulated the realm of ideas, which was the essence of things which we see in our material world. For example, the idea of a circle is more fundamental than all of the (imperfect) circles which we see in reality. Plato identified mathematics as one of those ideal planes of reality. The equation of a circle, he thought, is more perfect than any circle that exists

---

[4] http://www.sacred-texts.com/hin/rigveda/rv10129.htm

in physical space because you can calculate precisely the points of a circle using that equation (but they can never be physically located that precisely because matter is discontinuous). This idea reaches beyond our sensory universe to a more spiritual realm.

If we see the universe as an expression of divine thought, then we might think of God as a scientist who is experimenting on the forms of matter that are possible. George Coyne argues that science "reveals a God who made a universe that has within it a certain dynamism and thus participates in the very creativity of God."[5] It could be that God has created a universe in which scientific laws are operating in a way that brings forth unexpected outcomes. In that case, God might be surprised by the course that this universe takes (and maybe there are other universes with different laws that take another course).

Where did nature come from?

Give me, O God, to sing that thought!
Give me—give him or her I love, this quenchless faith
In Thy ensemble. Whatever else withheld, withhold not from us,
Belief in plan of Thee enclosed in Time and Space.
Walt Whitman, "Song of the Universal"

Many verses in the Qur'an emphasize the way that nature shows the power and majesty of God: "It is he who made the sun a shining radius" (Qur'an 10:5); "God keeps the heavens and the earth from vanishing" (Qur'an 35:41). These are good examples of basic religious affirmations rather than scientific statements. In the Muslim mystical tradition, "Sufi authors beautifully and poetically evoke the divine in and through nature."[6] Muslim

---

[5] George Coyne, *Faith and Knowledge: Towards a New Meeting of Science and Theology* (Libreria Editrice Vaticana, 2007), 44.
[6] Philip Clayton, *Religion and Science: The Basics* (Routledge, 2013), 51.

thinkers like Seyyed Hossein Nasr have tried to understand "the 'vertical cause' of all things, along with the horizontal, a science that issues from and returns to the Real (al-Haqq), Who is the Cause of all things."[7] This statement shows the kind of theological thinking about religious scriptures that examines the foundational ideas of the religion.

Some Muslims claim that scientific ideas can be found embedded in scriptures long before the scientific theories were proclaimed. For example, the Qur'an says: "He is the One who created the night and the day, and the sun and the moon; each floating in its own orbit" (Qur'an 21:33). Maurice Bucaille interpreted these images as proto-scientific ideas that were later confirmed by scientific investigation.[8] Muzaffar Iqbal says that "Bucaille attempted to show that the Qur'an contains scientifically correct information about the creation of the heavens and earth, human reproduction, and certain other aspects of the natural world"[9] but that this is a "stretch [of] Qur'anic hermeneutics."[10] For example, some verses are a little harder to reconcile: "It is God who created seven heavens and a similar number of earths" (Qur'an 65:12).

Similarly, the Sikh religion is fond of witnessing to the power of one God. Their scriptures have some fascinating images:

> There are hundreds of thousands of nether worlds, and hundreds of thousands of skies. ...It cannot be possible to count ...
> Because the accounting person may reach the end of his

---

[7] Ibid., 48.
[8] Maurice Bucaille, *The Bible, the Qur'an and Science: The Holy Scriptures Examined in the Light of Modern Knowledge* (Elmhurst, N.Y.: Tahrike Tarsile Qurán, 2003).
[9] Muzaffar Iqbal, *Contemporary Issues in Islam and Science* V. 2 (Ashgate, Surrey, 2012), xiii.
[10] Ibid., xiv.

life during counting,
It will still be incomplete.
Guru Nanak says that God is Great
Who knows the account (of the celestial bodies in the universe).
(Guru Granth Sahib, M1, Jap 22, p. 5)[11]

These images present a realistic picture of the cosmos but they don't really give a detailed hypothesis in the scientific sense.

In the more contemplative approach of the Eastern religions there seems to be more flexibility to read the texts metaphorically as an understanding of the foundations of reality. For example, the Buddhist notion of interdependence is more a metaphysical statement about the underlying structure of reality (even deeper than scientific descriptions). The Chinese monk Taixu says: "Science does not go far enough into the mysteries of Nature, and if she went further the Buddhist doctrine would be even more evident."[12] For example, in Buddhism individuals are seen as having no permanent identity because they are a constant flux of inter-related causal factors. If we pursued this line of thought scientifically, we might end up with a more Buddhist view of the person.

Similarly, in Buddhism the universe is seen as having no single cause (such as a creator god) but instead arises from a network of intersecting influences. Donald S. Lopez, Jr. says that "Buddha described a universe that was not created by God but that functioned according to laws of cause and effects."[13] This follows "the principle of 'Dependent Arising' ('this being given, that arises'). All things arise out of all else; they are neither separate atoms nor the product of a single creator God."[14] The idea of "nothingness" (*sunyata*) is developed exhaustively in

---

[11] http://sikhinstitute.org/akal_takht08/hardsi.html
[12] John Hedley Brooke and Ronald Numbers, eds., *Science and Religion around the World* (Oxford University Press, 2012), 218.
[13] Ibid., 215.
[14] Clayton, *Religion and Science: The Basics*, 99.

Buddhist philosophy. It means that our everyday conception that things exist is an illusion because there is nothing constant. Everything changes because every single thing is caught up in a network of interacting forces.

Buddhism thus does not view the world as a creation by God. The Dalai Lama says "Buddhism and science share a fundamental reluctance to postulate a transcendent being as the origin of all things."[15] Buddhist views of the universe see it as an intersection of causes without a creator making it happen. This view seems more compatible with scientific explanations of the origins of the universe.

Does science challenge belief?

Religion is an illusion and it derives its strength from the fact that it falls in with our instinctual desires.
Sigmund Freud

This survey of religious attitudes towards science will begin with an overview of the methods of each discipline and the history of their interaction. Then we can get into the issues: we will start with evolution because it has been such a firestorm of controversy. Charles Darwin's studies of natural changes in animal populations fueled the growing passion for scientific discovery. Many interpreted these theories about human beings without recourse to supernatural causes. The battles between creationists and evolutionists have polarized the two communities, with many holding to the assumption that the two are incompatible (if one is right, the other is wrong).

In the field of biology, the discovery of DNA and the role of genetics further consolidated the hold of evolutionary theory. This theoretical advance must be set within the growing

---

[15] Dalai Lama XIV, *The Universe in a Single Atom: The Convergence of Science and Spirituality* (New York: Morgan Road Books, 2005), 84.

clamour of the environmental movement, which studies the large contexts in which life moves, the great cycles of our planet. As well, both of these developments bring the ethical dimensions of our increasing knowledge to the fore, requiring a religious response rather than one of the intellect alone.

In the 21st century, there is gradually a greater acceptance of the possibility for science and faith to live beside each other, perhaps still in conflict at times, but often serving the same purpose. In part, this uneasy truce has come about because of a new humility on the part of science. In physics, although great strides have been made through the theories of Einstein, Bohr and others, the basic elements of the universe seem to remain mysterious. Heisenberg's "uncertainty principle" also sheds doubt on the ability of human beings to discover the fundamental nature of matter, since observing this deep-down level seems to modify it by that very action.

Some theologians have welcomed the theories of the new physics since they seem to open up a new space in which to talk about God. These theories will be discussed in terms of how they allow us to think about the way in which God continues to sustain the world. If the fundamental structure of our universe is open-ended, we can more easily conceive of God upholding the process of the cosmos, instead of seeing it running on inexorable laws (without any further intervention). Granted, this does not leave much scope for God's action, if God can only intervene at the sub-atomic level.

The theories of Sigmund Freud sparked a re-examination of the traditional ways that theologians viewed the human being, especially our rational side. Reason was long held to be a hallmark of God's image imprinted on human beings, but Freud's theory of the unconscious fragmented our rational self and put into question the role of rationality. Further, his explanations of religion denigrated the role of faith in human thinking and feeling. Further psychological research has unearthed the social foundations of ethics. Putting this together with evolution, recent sociobiological theories propose an integrated view of the development of human consciousness and society in a way that seems to explain (and simultaneously undermine) the role of religion. Opening up the discussion to include the environment, some religious believers have seen the recent ecological movement as a source of reflection on God's role in our world.

Despite the continued perception that science and religion are fundamentally at odds, many theologians and scientists are writing about the interfaces between the two. A recent survey of American scientists reported that 40 per cent believe in God so perhaps the gulf is not as wide as it is perceived to be.[16] Alister McGrath argues that the church has ignored science for too long, thus relegating itself to intellectual bywaters. He suggests that nature should be seen as a source for theological thinking.[17] Controversies exist over how to interpret the scientific theories theologically. My contribution in the following pages will try to place this debate as broadly as possible by using the various religious voices on our planet. My perspective has mostly been formed by Christian theology so I will pursue examples from that perspective.

---

[16] E. J. Larson and L. Witham, "Scientists are Still Keeping the Faith," in *Nature* 386 (3 April 1997), 435-436. A more detailed report of a number of surveys can be found in the appendix in Larry Witham, *Where Darwin Meets the Bible: Creationists and Evolutionists in America* (Oxford University Press, 2002).

[17] Alister McGrath, *A Scientific Theology* Vol 1: *Nature*; Vol. 2: *Reality*; Vol. 3; *Theory* (London: Continuum and Grand Rapids, MI: Eerdman's), 2001-3.

Methodological considerations

My comprehension of God comes from the deeply felt conviction of a superior intelligence that reveals itself in the knowable world.
Albert Einstein

Both theology and science have deliberate procedures by which their reflection is guided. In science, the experimental method predominates: a hypothesis is made and tested in a repeatable manner. Careful observation of the world is combined with theoretical models tested by independent trials. In theology, thinking about the spiritual dimension of our lives is guided by traditional sources, especially the scriptures of the various religious traditions, but also the historical record of religious experience. Science and religion have different languages for talking about the world but the same issues can arise in each endeavor.

The vocabularies of science and religion are often quite distinct: one talks about matter and energy, the other about spirit and sacrament. Einstein thought that

>science can only ascertain what *is*, but not what *should be*, and outside of its domain value judgments of all kinds remain necessary. Religion, on the other hand, deals only with evaluations of human thought and

action: it cannot justifiably speak of facts and relationships between facts.[18]

Both, however, are concerned with truth, and both seek to understand this life in which we are enmeshed.

Above all, we should not confuse the two disciplines. St. Augustine realized this in his commentary on Genesis. He criticized those who interpret the scriptures as purporting to explain things scientifically. If readers take the poetic utterances of the holy books as fact, he asks:

> How are they going to believe those books in matters concerning the resurrection of the dead, the hope of eternal life, and the kingdom of heaven, when they think their pages are full of falsehoods on facts which they themselves have learnt from experience and the light of reason?[19]

To begin, then, let us make clear the methods of science and religion.

What is faith?

Our life is a faint tracing on the surface of mystery.
Annie Dillard, *Pilgrim at Tinker Creek*

"Religion" is a notoriously difficult word to define since there are such widely different examples of belief and practice. In order to compare religion and science, this book will focus on the intellectual activities of both. I will use the word "theology" in order to focus particular attention on the analysis of the ideas of a religion (and my foremost examples will be Christian because that is my background). Paulos Gregorios gives an excellent overview of the activity of believing in religions (he

---

[18] Albert Einstein, "Science and Religion" in Timothy Ferris, ed. *The World Treasury of Physics, Astronomy and Mathematics* (Little, Brown, 1981), 831.
[19] Augustine, "The Literal Meaning of Genesis" trans. John Hammond Taylor, S. J. *Ancient Christian Writers* 41 (Newman Press: 1982), 45.

uses a more fundamental word: faith). He argues that there are several misunderstandings of faith: first, "giving assent to what is proposed as dogma by the official magisterium of the Church"[20] and second, an "over-emphasis on the subjective element."[21] He draws attention to the activity of faith: "allowing oneself to be trustingly carried, nourished, supported, by God, and the consequent strengthening and transformation of human personality and society."[22] Faith is a relationship based on the shared characteristics of God and human beings.

Religious statements are called "beliefs" precisely because we cannot know for sure about the object of our belief. Faith takes the form of commitment and thus produces a way of life based on those assumptions. Keith Ward says: "Believers do not infer God as an absentee 'first cause', or construct God as a speculative theory. They seek to know and love a reality of supreme perfection."[23] Our actions are formed by our beliefs about the world, even though those beliefs might not be fully testable.

Science thus studies a reality that is enveloped in a deeper ground or cause. Ward argues that God is "the sustainer of a network of dynamic interrelated energies; and might well be seen as the ultimate environing non-material field which draws from material natures a range of the potentialities which lie implicit within them."[24] For example, in biology, evolution is a description of how life came to be (the best theory, at least for now, since it is coherent and with a very large scope, uniting evidence from various disciplines with grand explanatory power). Theology as a systematic discipline adds a foundational

---

[20] Paulos Gregorios, "Science and Faith: Complementary or Contradictory?" in Roger Shinn, ed. *Faith and Science in an Unjust World* Vol. 1 (Fortress Press, 1980), 47-8.
[21] Ibid., 48.
[22] Ibid., 49.
[23] Keith Ward, *God, Chance and Necessity* (Oneworld, 1996), 97.
[24] Ibid., 57.

principle that God is the one that creates (with great power and order, in a grand design—this explanation shows the incredible intelligence of God).

In the analysis that follows, I will focus on the intellectual structures that theology develops based on its foundational beliefs. It is clear that there are differences between the practices of religion (mostly centred around worship and ethics) and those of science (focused on the ways to know something about the world). They have very different ways of being in the world. However, in order to pursue some sort of dialogue, the ideas that ground these practices will be compared. I will confine my examination to the ideas contained in the two disciplines. For reasons of brevity, I will not be able to include consideration of religion as a cultural practice.

What is science?

In the temple of science are many mansions, and various indeed are they that dwell therein and the motives that have led them thither.
Albert Einstein

Science is a method of understanding the context of our lives, ever reaching for a more complete and accurate relation to what is around and inside us. There are other ways of understanding our existence, especially through art and literature. As well, the abstract and practical disciplines of morality, politics and economics are agreements about how we understand and thereby construct our social world. These may involve scientific considerations, but they take in a broader range of human interests and identity.

Science is a limited exercise, a conscious narrowing of vision, in order to precisely articulate a particular area in which we are interested. Scientists in movies are often stereotypically portrayed as 'absent-minded professors' since they are so preoccupied by their concentrated attention on one topic. By concentrating on what is available through their senses, scientists focus their attention on the tangible, material aspects of reality. Withholding their personal bias (or at least trying to), they aim to observe only that which is observable by anyone, anywhere. Science has a particularly rigorous language: precise description using distinct categories.

Science is seen to be objective: a neutral account of the way the world is. Because it is so successful, it tends to become a defining paradigm for all human knowledge. This attitude penetrates into the work of scientists, as they attempt to make their own discipline define the sum total of all existence (reducing all processes to interactions of atoms). Albert Einstein said: "One can have the clearest and most complete knowledge of what *is*, and yet not be able to deduct from that what should be the *goal* of our human aspirations."[25] Science can only show us what is; imagination can show us what could be.

Observation, however, is not completely objective. What scientists call a fact (something out there) is dependent to a certain degree on the mindset one brings to bear upon the external world. That is why scientists make a point of subjecting their findings to their peers, in order to independently verify them. Objectivity, then, as Del Ratzsch defines it, requires that "neutral, public, shared observational facts could be employed to settle disputes objectively and to objectively guide one away from incorrect theories."[26] Developing general theories should account for what everyone experiences and explain it in a way satisfactory to all.

Science is thus a limited exercise, a conscious narrowing of our vision to the particular and concrete. Ratzsch defines science as

---

[25] Albert Einstein, "Science and Religion" in Ferris, 829.
[26] Del Ratzsch, *Philosophy of Science: The Natural Sciences in Christian Perspective* (InterVarsity Press, 1986), 30.

> a theoretical explanatory discipline which objectively addresses natural phenomena within the general constraints that (1) its theories must be rationally connectable to generally specifiable empirical phenomena and that (2) it normally does not leave the natural realm for the concepts employed in its explanations.[27]

The theories of science provide causal frameworks in which to place the detailed observations of the world.

Karl Popper argued that scientific statements can be delineated from other kinds of language by their falsifiability.[28] Popper is famous for his criteria for distinguishing science from non-science. His proposal suggests that scientific statements have a 'yes' or 'no' answer, as opposed to those statements that are simply expressive of emotions. Therefore, pseudo-scientific statements (like astrology) can be identified. They are never falsified by any experience (supporters often engage in special pleading or selective use of evidence). Any scientific system must be tested empirically.

The most important procedure in science is the way that proposed hypotheses are tested. The method is familiar to anyone who has done an experiment in a high school science lab:

> From a new idea, put up tentatively, and not yet justified in any way—an anticipation, a hypothesis, a theoretical system, or what you will—conclusions are drawn by means of logical deduction. These conclusions are then compared with one another and with other relevant statements, so as to find what logical relations (such as equivalence, derivability, compatibility or incompatibility) exist between them.[29]

---

[27] Ratzsch, 15.
[28] Karl Popper, *The Logic of Scientific Discovery* (London: Hutchison, 1972), 40.
[29] Ibid., 32.

This hypothetico-deductive procedure aims to yield some certainty about conclusions reached by experiments. It is designed to disprove bad theories, leaving the good ones to survive.

Scientific theories are never completely proven because new observations might emerge from experiments. However, these theories are our best guess until a better theory comes along. What does this mean for theology? Is it ever falsifiable? Belief in God is so strong that nothing seems to shake the faith of strong believers. I would argue, however, that there are some empirical situations that might falsify theology. St. Paul says that if Christ were not raised from the dead, our faith would be in vain. If God does not exist, theology is meaningless. These things are not empirically discoverable, though. John Hick says that they are "eschatologically verifiable," meaning we will only find out when we die or this world ends.

Science, by definition, can only be testable in the human community by continuing investigations that are never finished (there is always more to discover). It might take a long time to conclusively demonstrate the trends in the data (a recent example would be the current theories about climate change). I would argue that our theology is also a human endeavor that is inter-subjectively tested (by a communal discernment of God's action in our midst). It is a human, fallible intellectual structure that we must always strive to inter-subjectively test with our experience.

Paul Tillich suggests that we understand the word 'science' in its larger sense. He argues: "there is another element in science: its participation in the whole of man's spiritual life and, therefore, in the self-interpretation of man in the universe."[30] In this way, science can be seen as the study of everything in its proper context, in the service of an understanding of the human person in the cosmos (made by

---

[30] Paul Tillich, *The Spiritual Situation in our Technical Society* (Macon, GA: Mercer University Press, 1988), 155.

God). Religion is systematic as well, but covers a larger context than science. Tillich delineates the differences:

> Science is the cognitive approach to the whole of finite objects, their interrelations and their processes. Religion is the total approach to that which gives meaning to our life and therefore, concerns us unconditionally and ultimately.[31]

Religion answers the big questions (like "why are we here?") whereas science gives details about what is here.

Conflicts arise, according to this view, "if science confuses its religious and metaphysical matrix with its methodologically gained results. Whenever this happens the scientist becomes a theologian."[32] For example, scientists might develop a framework for understanding our existence by elevating climate change to an apocalyptic scenario (we're causing the end of the world!). If so, they are explaining the larger reasons for climate change from a religious perspective.

Perceiving and interpreting data

What may be known about God is plain to them, because God has made it plain to them. For since the creation of the world God's invisible qualities—his eternal power and divine nature—have been clearly seen, being understood from what has been made, so that men are without excuse.
Romans 1: 19-20 (NIV)

Imagine that you are walking in the desert. You are tremendously thirsty but you see water in the distance. You keep walking but eventually you realize that you were seeing a mirage. All of our observations are like that in a way because we

---

[31] Ibid.
[32] Ibid.

have to interpret what our eyes give to us. Michael Polanyi argues that in all thinking there is always an element of personal judgement of the evidence.[33] Religious experiences are particularly notorious for this kind of personal interpretation. However, Janet Martin Soskice argues that "both scientific knowing and revelation have a bedrock in experience, observation and the observing community."[34] There are similar intellectual processes going on in the two disciplines.

Albert Einstein recounted his intellectual journey to the famous theories of relativity by describing the intuitive vision that allowed him to come up with a new way of looking at the world. He said: "I believe in intuition and inspiration. Imagination is more important than knowledge."[35] Del Ratzsch argues that "it takes an imaginative leap to go from a body of data to a theoretical account of that data."[36] The imaginative leap may start in the subjective mind of the theorist, but once formulated, it must be subject to other checks and balances.

However, the world seems to impose itself on human action and thought. There's a famous story about Newton discovering gravity because an apple fell on his head. More importantly, he measured the rate at which objects fall in order to come up with an equation that could measure the force of gravity. Alister McGrath suggests that "the natural sciences are founded on the perception of explicable regularity to the world, which is capable of being represented mathematically."[37] He continues with a caveat: "It could, of course, be argued that this

---

[33] Michael Polanyi, *Science, Faith and Society* (University of Chicago Press), 1964.
[34] Janet Martin Soskice, "Knowledge and Experience in Science and Religion: Can We be Realists?" in Robert John Russell *et al*, eds., *Physics, Philosophy and Theology: A Common Quest for Understanding* (Vatican Observatory, 1988), 173.
[35] Albert Einstein, *Cosmic Religion: With Other Opinions and Aphorisms* (Covici-Friede, 1931), 97.
[36] Ratzsch, 24.
[37] Alister McGrath, *The Foundations of Dialogue in Science and Religion* (Blackwell, 1998), 36.

perception of 'orderliness' reflects a propensity to discern patterns and impose coherence within the human mind, rather than any intrinsic structuring of the natural world itself."[38] The idea of gravity is not just a human invention.

Scientists are sometimes criticized for focusing so much on the details that they lose the larger picture. Jacob Bronowski puts it this way: "Nature is not a gigantic formalizable system. In order to formalize it, we have to make some assumptions which cut out some parts. We then lose the total connectivity."[39] Biologists study animals by dissecting them and so they may lose sight of how the animal interacts with its environment.

Models and metaphors

When we try to pick out anything by itself, we find that it is bound fast by a thousand invisible cords that cannot be broken, to everything in the universe.
John Muir

The interlocking spiral helix which Watson and Crick built in their laboratory illustrates well the way in which scientists construct physical models of the world which they are investigating. Ian Barbour defines a model as "a symbolic representation of selected aspects of the behaviour of a complex system for particular purposes."[40] In the Christian and Jewish religions, the poetry of the Old Testament gives many models of God such as the relation between king and subject, the craftsman and the artifact, and the lover and the beloved. Recently, feminist theologians have recommended new models of God (such as mother) in order to better understand the way that God relates to us. Each of these aspects of our human reality is applied

---

[38] Ibid., 37.
[39] Jacob Bronowski, *The Origins of Knowledge and Imagination* (New Haven: Yale University Press, 1978), 80.
[40] Ian Barbour, *Myths, Models and Paradigms.* (Harper and Row, 1974), 6.

metaphorically to God's existence. Religions do this by telling stories about God's action in the world. Of course, God is greater than anything we can imagine but we can only use concepts from our existence and stretch them beyond our reality to another dimension. This metaphorical extension of our reality to another kind of spiritual existence can explain the many religious depictions of this reality (using different words and metaphors).

The central model of Christian theology is the Trinity. It encapsulates the central elements of Christian revelation: creation, fall, redemption and grace (eschatology). In other words, Christians understand God by thinking about how Jesus relates to the abstract idea of a creator of this world. These themes intertwine throughout the multi-dimensional relationships between the three persons of the Trinity, but they also point to the one core concept that is embodied in God's being: personal relationship. Scientific models, in contrast, are developed by observation and experimentation. These models depends on the material reality of the objects observed (this sometimes descends into materialism) and the objectivity required by deductive testing of hypotheses (sometimes tending towards reductionism to the most basic level—atomism).

Religious models are often more verbal in character and thus take on a metaphorical character (especially in myths and poetry). Stories of creation often use metaphors derived from the natural world (like animals in aboriginal myths participating in the creation of the world). Metaphors bring two different images together in a way that provokes surprise. "Man is a wolf" brings out the similarities between ideas that seem at first glance to be distinct. Metaphors retain a tension between the similarities and differences forged by the juxtaposition of meaning from two different sources.[41] Ideas interact in a way that stretches the web of language, creating new ways of thinking. At the same time,

---

[41] See Janet Martin Soskice's analysis, *Metaphors in Religious Language* (Oxford University Press, 1987).

however, metaphors do not make the juxtaposed ideas the same. In fact, a good metaphor works because the two founding images retain their distinctive character. It is the relationship between disparate realms of existence that creates the power of metaphor. The title for this book suggests another metaphor for God: a scientist who has created the world as an experiment in freedom! Think about how the interaction of religion and science can illuminate our thinking about God.

The model of inter-personal communication is often used in religion, since God's revelation to us is like another person revealing their deepest hopes and dreams to us. Non-theistic religions are often seen as having a less personal notion of the spiritual dimension of existence. Nevertheless, each spirit still communicates with others, and we have to allow the other to be independent, trusting them to give something of themselves to us. Science may seem to be a much more impersonal activity than that, since it seeks to know objects and events rather than persons. But scientists also have to trust the world to display the sort of regularity that will allow them to describe it with some degree of certainty.

Paradigms

When I heard the learn'd astronomer;
When the proofs, the figures, were ranged in columns before me;
When I was shown the charts and the diagrams, to add, divide, and measure them;
When I, sitting, heard the astronomer, where he lectured with much applause in the lecture-room,
How soon, unaccountable, I became tired and sick;
Till rising and gliding out, I wander'd off by myself,
In the mystical moist night-air, and from time to time,
Look'd up in perfect silence at the stars.
Walt Whitman, *Leaves of Grass*

Thomas Kuhn argued that science operates according to paradigms: "the entire constellation of beliefs, values, techniques, and so on shared by the members of a given community."[42] Einstein had to convince others captivated by the Newtonian paradigm that time and space are relative. Kuhn says that "Paradigms gain their status because they are more successful than their competitors in solving a few problems that the group of practitioners has come to recognize as acute."[43] Paradigms change because somebody like Einstein comes up with a better framework (when new evidence is discovered). In the next section, the history of science will be portrayed as a succession of paradigms when a new theory forces us to re-evaluate our world.

Hans Küng draws a parallel between this view of science and theological method. He argues that science is "a process of continuous change and development."[44] Theories like Einstein's idea of relativity require rethinking the whole structure of ideas. Similarly, in theology, "new hypotheses and theories emerge as a result of a highly complex and generally protracted replacement of a hitherto accepted model of interpretation or 'paradigm' by a new one."[45] Both science and theology are interpretations of reality that need to be revised periodically:

> We speak of a 'model' as 'paradigm' in order to stress also the provisional character of the project, which in fact holds only under certain assumptions and within certain limits; which does not in principle exclude other

---

[42] Thomas Kuhn, *The Structure of Scientific Revolutions* (University of Chicago Press, 1970), 175.
[43] Ibid., 23.
[44] Hans Küng, "Paradigm Change in Theology: A Proposal for a Discussion," in Hans Kung and David Tracy, eds., *Paradigm Change in Theology: A Symposium for the Future* (Edinburgh: T & T Clark, 1989), 6.
[45] Ibid., 7.

projects, but always grasps reality only comparatively objectively, in a particular perspectivity and variability.[46]

While it is true that reality is observed from different perspectives, it should also be noted that science strives for some agreement about the reality as represented by a communal consensus.

Because there are so many different religions, we might see them as paradigms that develop their own view of the spiritual realm. Küng draws the parallel more closely:

> Like natural science, the theological community has a 'normal science' with its classical authors, textbooks and teachers, which is characterized by a cumulative growth of knowledge, by a solution of remaining problems ('puzzles'), and by resistance to everything that might result in a changing or replacement of the established paradigm.[47]

Both science and religion have sources that dictate which interpretations are valid. For science, this is the data of the physical world. For theology, it is revelation interpreted through human experience. As an example, the Protestant Reformation re-interpreted the Christian tradition using a new understanding of the primary sources (especially Jesus' words). Intriguingly, many different Christian churches were formed through this process. In contrast, scientists are supposed to agree upon their findings.

Theology, it seems to me, should not be divorced from the praxis of scientists engaged in the interpretation of the world. Our inferences about the causes of phenomena are embedded in a framework of assumptions about the way the world is. Newton had to come up with the theory of gravity in the face of standard thinking about why the stars and planets moved the way they do. Wentzel van Huyssteen argues that there are "no universal

---

[46] Ibid., 10.
[47] Ibid., 14.

standards of rationality against which we can measure other beliefs or research traditions."[48] However, it is possible to do "cross-contextual evaluation"[49] of our networks of ideas and theories. This interdisciplinary conversation requires a foot in both worlds and an understanding of the methodologies of both science and theology.

Experiment

Ask the animals, and they will teach you; the birds of the air, and they will tell you; ask the plants of the earth, and they will teach you; and the fish of the sea will declare to you. Who among all these does not know that the hand of the Lord has done this?
Job 12:7-10

Science and religion proceed from different sources and are guided by distinct sets of normative judgments. Although both are related to our experience of life, different techniques of understanding are brought to bear upon the complexity of existence. Religious belief relies on a community of interpretation steeped in the history of experiences of people, as recorded in the Scripture and other writings. Science also relies on a public forum of accountability, whereby individual observations and theories can be tested to remove subjective bias.

The public nature of community is important to theology as well. An early Christian formula for the catholic (meaning universal) church stated: "that which has been believed everywhere, always and by all."[50] The inter-testability of faith is

---

[48] Wentzel van Huyssteen, *Duet or Duel? Theology and Science in a Postmodern World* (Trinity Press, 1998), 29.
[49] Ibid., 30.
[50] Vincent of Lerins, *Commonitorium*. http://www.newadvent.org/fathers/3506.htm

important to the worldwide church, all under God. Similarly, the Muslim principle of *ijma* emphasizes that the community should agree on what should be believed. Muhammed is reported to have said: "My community will never agree on an error."[51] The worldwide Muslim community is like an experiment in the experience of faith because it tests its beliefs and actions by comparing them with others in the community. It might take a while to reform bad practices and there might be pressure to conform but it seems to be a self-correcting enterprise.

Both science and faith depend on individual experience: the scientist in the laboratory, the believer at worship and in prayer. Both, in a sense, must subject their experience to the corporate body, although heretics will appear in both camps. The truly revolutionary aspect of modern science is its dedication to experiment. The ability to repeat the results of other scientists is crucial to the scientific method. Similarly, the Buddha famously said: "You must be your own lamps, be your own refuges. Take refuge in nothing outside yourselves. Hold firm to the truth as a lamp and a refuge."[52] Buddhism follows his principle by encouraging individuals to experiment in their own meditation techniques.

Although religion seems to be unfalsifiable in principle, there are some cases that provide an environment for testing the claims of believers. The problem of evil is one such counter-argument. The hypothesis that God is good and loving and all-powerful seems to be falsified by the experiment of this world, where evil seems to be all too prevalent. Christian theologians typically say that this hypothesis needs to include the variable of freedom. Evil happens because human beings choose badly.

Another area of experiment lies in the realm of prayer. There are currently experiments in which patients in hospitals

---

[51] From a hadith (reported sayings of Muhammed) http://en.wikipedia.org/wiki/Ijma.
[52] http://www.globalcultures.net/sacred/Life%20of%20Buddha-Part2.htm

are prayed for (and others in a control group are not) and the results compared. A double-blind study found no significant difference between the two groups. [53] Further, there was no placebo effect: in fact, quite the opposite. A third group that knew they were being prayed for experienced more complications than both of the other groups. [54] David Myers criticized the methodology of this experiment and predicted a null result, citing among other factors the 'noise level' of other prayers being prayed for both groups by persons unknown to the experimenters. [55]

This kind of experiment is theologically flawed, for it reduces God to a cause among other causes. It is like the experiment that weighs a human body just before and after death. A slight difference in weight is interpreted as the soul escaping the body but by definition the soul is immaterial and has no weight! Prayer is by definition a profound kind of communication with a God who deigns to act in this world in ways that go beyond our comprehension. Myers argues that "God works not in the gaps of what we don't yet understand, but in and through nature, including the healing ministries that led people of faith to introduce medicine and hospitals worldwide."[56] The experimental design, thus, cannot put God to the test by examining the consequences of prayers. If we use the metaphor of "God as scientist," we could see prayer as an experiment that God runs on us. In this scenario, God creates a universe with free creatures and then waits to see what they will do.

---

[53] See Russell Stannard, "The Prayer Experiment: Does Prayer Work?" *Second Opinion* 2 (January 2000); also in *The God Experiment* (Faber and Faber, 1999).

[54] Herbert Benson, et al., "Study of the Therapeutic Effects of Intercessory Prayer (STEP) in Cardiac Bypass Patients" *American Heart Journal* 151(4):934-942, April 2006.

[55] David G. Myers, "Is Prayer Clinically Effective?" in *Reformed Review*, 2000. http://www.davidmyers.org/Brix?pageID=53

[56] Ibid.

Religion and science: history

For the Creator, who is the very source of astronomy and, as Plato wrote, 'practices eternal geometry,' does not stray from his own archetype.
Johannes Kepler

Some historians of science argue that Christian thought acted as a seedbed for scientific questioning (since it encourages scientists to examine what kind of world God created). It is perhaps unfair to cast the history of the development of science in this way because the definition of scientific method that arose in Western universities relegates other thinkers (especially those nurtured by religions other than Christianity) to an intellectual backwater. Recent examinations of the development of science around the world have shown that the relationship between science and religion has developed in various ways (the 'complexity' thesis).[57] I will include a few examples of developments of scientific thinking in other cultures but I cannot exhaustively examine the historical development of these ideas.

Throughout the history of Christian theology there have been thinkers who have been well-versed in both science and theology (for example, Newton, Pascal, and Darwin). In the

---

[57] See Yiftach Fehige, ed. *Science and Religion: East and West* (Routledge: 2016). He credits John Hedley Brooke with spearheading this thesis.

middle ages, monasteries contained treasuries of knowledge (including the proto-scientific thinking of the Greek philosophers) and the church began the cathedral schools that would develop into the first universities in Europe. In the pages that follow, I will trace the development of Western science as an example of intellectual development in the context of a religious culture. The question of scientific method serves as a useful analytical example in order to examine the development of science within a religious context.

Already in the early Christian era, Augustine gave a wonderful example of the way that Christians should read the Bible with an inquiring spirit, comparing the metaphors of revelation with those of science. He questions the text and tries to extract the essential meaning. In the case of Genesis, it is difficult to determine how to take this account of the origin of the universe. He notes that there are different possible interpretations:

> In all the sacred books, we should consider the eternal truths that are taught, the facts that are narrated, the future events that are predicted, and the precepts or counsels that are given. In the case of a narrative of events, the question arises as to whether everything must be taken according to the figurative sense only, or whether it must be expounded and defended also as a faithful record of what happened. No Christian will dare say that the narrative must not be taken in a figurative sense.[58]

Augustine struggled with interpreting the first chapters of Genesis as accurately as possible. He was not opposed to a figurative interpretation, but did try to stay faithful to the plain sense of the Scriptures, inasmuch as he could reconcile that with his common sense and the science of the day. For example, he

---

[58] Augustine, "The Literal Meaning of Genesis," trans. John Hammond Taylor, S. J. *Ancient Christian Writers* 41 (Newman Press, 1982), 19.

tried to understand how it could be possible that light was created before the sun (which only appeared on the fourth day). Augustine does not read the Scripture as if it has the answers lying ready to hand. He uses his mind to question what it might mean. In the end, he reads the Bible through theological principles such as the transcendence of God and the Trinitarian activity in this universe. We should not ask Scripture to answer questions it does not even consider, but instead read it for the wisdom it contains about our intended relation to God.

Augustine realized that the Genesis account is not giving a straightforward description of events. The origin of the world is beyond human knowledge. He cautions:

> Above all, let us remember, as I have tried in many ways to show, that God does not work under the limits of time by motions of body and soul, as do men and angels, but by the eternal, unchangeable, and fixed exemplars of His coeternal Word and by a kind of brooding action of His equally coeternal Holy Spirit.[59]

His interpretation of this text is constantly guided by theological principles garnered from the rest of the Bible. The account in Genesis gives us a picture of God's creative activity, not a scientific description of the universe.

Augustine did not have a lot of empirical basis for his questioning. Hundreds of years later, Muslim astronomers were charting the astronomical movements in order to more accurately predict the advent of their religious festivals. Ibn al-Haytham "provided an inventory of the theoretical inconsistencies of the Ptolemaic models."[60] New theories were starting to be considered in order to explain apparent anomalies. Ibn al-Shatir proposed "combinations of perfect circular motions, with each

---

[59] Ibid., 41.
[60] Ahmad S. Dallal, "Early Islam" in John Hedley Brooke and Ronald Numbers, *Science and Religion around the World*, 126.

circle rotating uniformly around its center."⁶¹ However, most Muslim astronomers still assumed that the earth was at the centre (following Aristotle).

Other religions focused on the causal interactions of the universe rather than asking where they came from. Donald Lopez says that "Buddha described a universe that was not created by God but that functioned according to laws of cause and effects."⁶² Some imaginative reconstruction of the science of his day led to theological proposals by the Buddha: "He described multiple universes, each with its own sun, universes that arose out of nothingness and returned to nothingness over the course of vast cosmic phases of creation, abiding and disintegration."⁶³ This idea is actually common to many religions, especially when they see everything coming from a spiritual source (which as spirit is not a thing).

Some Buddhists have tried to connect their religious doctrines to the observational constraints of science. Taixu was a Chinese monk who was confident about the connections which would be realized: "Science does not go far enough into the mysteries of Nature, and if she went further the Buddhist doctrine would be even more evident."⁶⁴ This approach typifies the way that Buddhism is very attentive to the structures of the mind.

Another approach, typical to Hinduism, puts a theological scaffolding on the scientific structure, thus placing the theory in a religious context. Carl Sagan says:

> There is the deep and appealing notion that the universe is but a dream of the gods, who after a hundred Brahma years, dissolves himself into a dreamless sleep. The universe dissolves with him—until, after another

---

[61] Ibid., 127.
[62] Donald S. Lopez, Jr. "Buddhism" in Brooke and Numbers, 215.
[63] Ibid.
[64] Ibid., 218.

Brahma century, he stirs, recomposes himself and begins to dream the cosmic dream.[65]

Amit Goswami describes the implication of this view: "the unity of all subjects (Atman) in a single, all-encompassing consciousness or awareness (Brahman)."[66] We are in the mind of Brahman! If we see the world this way, science would become the self-reflection of the mind of God.

Medieval pre-scientific thinking

I sing the goodness of the Lord that filled the earth with food.
God formed the creatures with a word, and then pronounced them good.
Lord, how thy wonders are displayed, where'er I turn my eye,
if I survey the ground I tread, or gaze upon the sky.
Isaac Watts

In the late middle ages, explanations of observed events followed a pattern established by the ancient Greeks (whose texts were re-discovered in the thirteenth century having been preserved by Arab philosophers). Aristotle, who was so revered that he was often referred to as "the Philosopher," was a keen observer of nature. The roots of the scientific method lie in his careful description of what he saw.

Some of Aristotle's explanations may sound quaint to our ears. For example, he thought that stones fall to the ground because they are seeking their natural resting-place, the centre of the cosmos. This internal *telos* should not be seen as a subjective state but as fulfilling the natural order of the universe. In a way, this explanation does not explain anything, since it simply puts

---

[65] From Carl Sagan's film series *Cosmos*, quoted in Philip Clayton, *Religion and Science: The Basics* (Routledge, 2011), 68-69.
[66] Clayton, 80.

the description of the event inside the object (the falling-down activity of stones is made into a definition of the nature of stones). This mode of explanation, though, was extremely influential for the next millennium.

Even in our time, the notion of an orderly universe grips the popular imagination. Aristotle's attempt to describe all events as exhibitions of universal laws is a foundation of modern science. We may disagree with the laws of nature which he came up with but our approach is basically the same. Christians in the Middle Ages certainly did not see this idea as counter to faith. The idea of an orderly universe fit quite nicely into the theological conception of a world designed and sustained by God (although many Christian theologians retained Plato's conception of this relation, in which God's mind contains the ideal of this world, never actually reached here).

In the history of theology there is good warrant for seeing an imaginative creativity at work, understood as the work of God. Edward Grant shows how medieval theologians took the science of their day and worked at seeing it through theological eyes. Sometimes this approach ran counter to Aristotle's explanations:

> Various elements in Aristotle's philosophy were relevant to theology, most notably his conviction that the world is eternal: that it had no beginning and would never have an end. Aristotle could find no convincing argument for supposing that our world could have come into being naturally from any prior state of existence. For if the world came from a previously existing material thing, say B, we would then have to inquire from whence did B come, and so on through an infinite regression, since it

was assumed that the world could not have come from nothing.[67]
Aristotle thus concluded that the world is eternal, a conclusion uncongenial to Christian thought. The Christian doctrine of *creatio ex nihilo* (creation from nothing) posits a finite world.

Aristotle's view is not only a restriction on God's power but a restriction on God's will (after all, God might be able to do these things but still choose not to do them), to which Muslim scientists also objected. Al-Ghazali, in particular, wrote a diatribe entitled "The Incoherence of the Philosophers" in which he mocked those who pursue "theoretical inquiries which are the outcome of stumbling—skeptically, misguidedly and stupidly—upon fanciful notions."[68] He was not arguing against observations of the universe (such as eclipses) explained by philosophers but against their metaphysical thesis that temporal things like our world cannot come from an eternal source. On the other hand, ibn Sina (in the Latin West known as Avicenna) "believed that there exists a single set of principles that can explain the nature of the physical world, the reason for its creation and the relationship between mind and body."[69] He thought that these principles can be found if we look for them because Allah created a world that is orderly.

Grant argues that Christian theology provided a particularly hospitable framework for science to develop. Many theologians have considered the "book of nature" as a second revelation, subordinate to Scripture, but revealing something about God. Several historians have pointed out the deep roots of modern science not only in scientists who were devout Christians, but also in the theological mindset of those believers.

---

[67] Edward Grant, "Aristotle and Aristotelianism" in Gary Ferngren, ed. *Science and Religion: A Historical Introduction* (Johns Hopkins University Press, 2002), 35.
[68] Al-Ghazali, "Incoherence of the Philosophers" trans. Sabih Ahmad Kamali, Pakistan Philosophical Congress, 1958.
[69] Ehsan Masoud, *Science and Islam: A History.* Icon Books, 2009, 106-7.

In any case, science had a tendency to shake loose from the church's grasp, even a genial one which simply saw nature as a secondary source for theological reflection. In the thirteenth century, the Catholic church condemned statements of Aristotle as heretical.[70] Grant explains:

> Scattered through the works of Aristotle were propositions and conclusions demonstrating the natural impossibility of certain phenomena. For example, Aristotle had shown that it was impossible for a vacuum to occur naturally inside or outside the world, and he had also demonstrated the impossibility that other worlds might exist naturally beyond ours. Theologians came to view these Aristotelian claims of natural impossibility as restrictions on God's absolute power to do as he pleased.[71]

Christian medieval theologians asked: "why should an omnipotent God not be able to produce a vacuum inside or outside the world, if he chose to do so?"[72] But the point is not whether God can do something or not. The real question is: what has God done? The answer is not obvious. The only way to find out is to go out and look. Grant says:

> By appeal to the concept of God's absolute power, medieval natural philosophers introduced subtle and imaginative questions that often generated novel responses. By conceding that God could create other worlds, they inquired about the nature of those worlds.[73]

Because of their religious belief, scientists had "the profound sense that all of these activities were legitimate and important, that discovering the way the world operated was a laudable

---

[70] https://en.wikipedia.org/wiki/Condemnations_of_1210%E2%80%931277
[71] Grant, 40. See also John Hedley Brooke and Ronald Numbers, *Science and Religion around the World*, 74.
[72] Ibid., 40.
[73] Ibid., 41.

undertaking."[74] In this way, the inquiry of science was founded on theological foundations.

Alfred North Whitehead claimed that "the faith in the possibility of science, generated antecedently to the development of modern scientific theory, is an unconscious derivative from medieval theology."[75] Whitehead was a philosopher, not a historian, so his claims needed confirmation in actual historical events. Robert Merton took up the challenge and investigated 17th century England. He found that a majority of the Royal Society (the leading scientists of the day) were Puritan. Merton argued that the Puritan dedication to following God's vocation here on earth led to scientific progress. He claimed: "Experiment was the scientific expression of the practical, active, and methodical bent of the Puritans."[76] Many critiques of Merton's thesis have been published, pointing out that other social factors are at least as important as the faith of these scientists.

Nevertheless, even if religious faith is one factor among many, we can investigate what kind of faith would spur scientific research. R. G. Collingwood laid out the philosophical presuppositions behind this attitude. In his *Essay on Metaphysics*, he argued:

> Christianity, by maintaining that God is omnipotent and that the world of nature is a world of God's creating, completely altered the situation. It became a matter of faith that the world of nature should be regarded no longer as the realm of imprecision but as the realm of precision.[77]

---

[74] Ibid., 44.
[75] Quoted by Peter Hodgson in *Science and Belief in the Nuclear Age* (Sapientia Press of Ave Maria University, 2006), 30. Other expressions of this viewpoint include Rodney Stark, *For the Glory of God* (Princeton, 2004) and Willis Glover, *Biblical Origins of Modern Secular Culture: An Essay in the Interpretation of Western History* (Mercer University Press, 1984).
[76] Eugene Klaaren, *Religious Origins of Modern Science (*Eerdman's, 1977), 8.
[77] Ibid. 12, quoting Collingwood, *Essay on Metaphysics* (Oxford, 1940*)*, 253.

Peter Hodgson shows this theme operative in the middle ages: "Matter is ordered and rational because it was created by a rational God. We read in the book of Wisdom that the Creator ordered everything in measure, number and weight, which was the most often quoted biblical phrase in medieval times."[78] Christian theology can be seen to support scientific research, although it might not demand such action, given the many other concerns of the faith.

    The rise of science in Christian Europe may be in part a historical accident brought about by the confluence of many contributing factors. We can nevertheless investigate what Christianity contributed to the mix of social causes for the rise of a particular way of analyzing and investigating experience. Eugene Klaaren links this intellectual method to the conception of God's will evidenced in creation emphasized by John Duns Scotus (1266-1308). God is free to create in any way, not bound by our rational concepts. Thus, we must dare to be surprised by nature rather than limiting the act of God's creativity. Klaaren argues:

> Within this dialectical orientation, the order of creation was conceived in terms of law, and entities subject to law, rather than in terms of symbols with varying degrees of mind and soul which participated in the divine Logos. ... In principle, law was dependent chiefly upon God's will rather than His reason, although the latter was not neglected.[79]

Reason is necessary in order to discover and formulate the general laws (and new data might force them to be reformulated).

    Scotus emphasized the 'thisness' of things rather than an abstract essence. Rather than universal essences materialized in substances, nature displays a multitude of individual things.

---

[78] Hodgson, 26.
[79] Klaaren, 36.

This ontological view requires an inductive pattern of thinking. Harold Nebelsick sums it up this way:

> For science to begin, nature had to be seen as dependable, intrinsically worthwhile and knowable. It had to be understood in terms of a contingent rationality appropriate to it rather than in terms of a divine rationality that penetrated it.[80]

Rather than deducing the character or action of a thing from its principles, one must observe how that thing acts and formulate general principles.

Muslim theologians were also dedicated to finding the way that God's will is expressed in creation. Gaz Ahmed Muhtar Pasha says that "the verses on cosmic events (later called 'cosmic verses') in the Holy Qur'an, which is revealed by God, should be congruent with the truth attained by modern sciences."[81] There were Muslim scholars observing the motions of the stars and the planets in order to figure out what kind of universe Allah had created. There were even formulations of the empirical method by Ibn al-Haytham (born in Iraq in A.D. 965) although he is "sometimes described with a bit of exaggeration as 'the father of the scientific method' for his insistence on empiricism."[82] Taner Edis argues that "A few Muslim thinkers came close to developing a modern concept of experiment, but their work, at the periphery of the larger Muslim intellectual community as was so often the case, never put down roots."[83] Perhaps the focus on the transcendent reality made it less of a priority to focus on this world and how it works. Muzaffar Iqbal says that

---

[80] Harold P. Nebelsick, *The Renaissance, the Reformation and the Rise of Science.* (Edinburgh: T&T Clark, 1992), 156.
[81] Ekmeleddin Ihsanoglu, "Modern Islam" in John Hedley Brooke and Ronald Numbers, *Science and Religion around the World*, 168.
[82] Nidhal Guessoum, "Issues and Agendas of Islam and Science" in *Zygon* 47 (June 2012), 377.
[83] Taner Edis, *An Illusion of Harmony: Science and Religion in Islam* (Prometheus Books, 2007), 49.

> the unity of existence is a recurrent theme of the Qur'an that relates it to its central concept of Tawhid, the unicity of God. Thus linked ontologically with the realm of the divine, the realm of nature becomes more than the physical entity that it is; it becomes a sign ... pointing to a transcendent reality beyond itself.[84]

There was also considerable political turmoil in the Muslim empires which did not always allow theoretical exploration to be developed. There were many other factors contributing to the rise of science in Europe including the specialization of the medieval guilds, the political ambitions of monarchs and the Renaissance recovery of the individualistic ethos of the Greek philosophers.

The rise of modern science

I do not think it is necessary to believe that the same God who has given us our senses, reason, and intelligence wished us to abandon their use, giving us by some other means the information that we could gain through them.
Galileo Galilei

The new scientific method gave rise to a naturalistic framework for investigating reality. Medieval thinkers like Robert Grosseteste investigated how the eye sees colour. Francis Bacon laid the groundwork for the scientific method of investigation. He outlined what he considered to be the correct way to approach nature in order to understand it. Bacon considered science, or, as he called it, natural philosophy, to be the cornerstone of his new method for achieving certainty. He thought that it was

---

[84] Muzaffar Iqbal, "Traditional Islam and Modern Science" in Ted Peters and Gaymon Bennett, eds. *Bridging Science and Religion* (Fortress 2003), 150.

> after the word of God, at once the surest medicine against superstition and the most approved nourishment for faith, and therefore she is rightly given to religion as her most faithful handmaid, since the one displays the will of God, the other his power.[85]

He distinguished between the roles of faith and science but the rest of his work goes on without much mention of God.

Bacon represents the impulse of science to overcome the ignorance produced by the 'idols,' as he calls them, of the tribe and of religion. He says:

> There is a great difference between the Idols of the human mind and the Ideas of the divine. That is to say, between certain empty dogmas, and the true signatures and marks set upon the works of creation as they are found in nature.[86]

In the seventeenth century, investigations into the natural world gradually became more independent of the church. This tendency may have been linked to the Reformation, which loosened the hold of the church on many aspects of society.

In Italy, although Galileo Galilei was condemned by the church for drawing heretical conclusions from his observations, he did not consider his scientific views to be in conflict with the Bible. Galileo was educated at the University of Pisa, where he became professor in 1589.[87] He disagreed with Aristotelian theories of motion (that heavier things fall faster than light things) and so performed experiments with inclined planes (not, as legend has it, by dropping objects from the leaning tower). He

---

[85] Francis Bacon, *The New Organon and Related Writings*, ed. by Fulton Anderson (New York: Liberal Arts Press, 1960), 88-9.
http://www.constitution.org/bacon/nov_org.htm
[86] Ibid., 44.
[87] The following summary follows Richard Blackwell, "Galileo Galilei" in Gary Ferngren, *Science and Religion: A Historical Introduction* (Johns Hopkins University Press, 2002).

was a new breed of human being: a scientist. He sought truth through our senses, not relying on any traditional authority.

His fellow countryman, Leonardo da Vinci, painted a picture that represents man as the one who is a microcosm of the cosmos, measuring with his body the structures of the universe ("Vitruvian Man"). The Reformation, although promulgating the individual conscience, still rested in the faith of 'sola scriptura.' Luther, for example, condemned Copernicus because of scriptural objections such as Joshua 10:12-13 (where God stops the sun in its motion in order to lengthen the day).[88]

The Catholic church was relying on the science of its day. Aristotle thought that perfect spheres were surrounded by the *Primum Mobile* (the outermost sphere of the heavens). He thought the earth is at the centre because he saw the sun move, not the earth. Ptolemy proposed an alternative: a perfect circle revolves around a point offset from the unmoving earth, and an epicycle explains retrograde motion (the planets appear to go backwards in the sky at times). Copernicus retained the notion of perfect circles, but put the sun at the centre. Galileo still held with perfect circles and epicycles and did not follow Kepler's ellipses. All of the models were mathematical attempts to reconcile the data but Galileo used a telescope to find new evidence: the moons of Jupiter, craters on the moon, and sunspots (all disproving tenets of the Ptolemaic system).

Galileo argued that Scripture is valid unless "contrary physical argument is demonstrative."[89] The church wanted to treat the Copernican view as just a hypothesis. One of the leading church theologians, Cardinal Bellarmine, held that the Scriptural testimony of a fixed earth was primary. Galileo responded that Augustine held that the Bible did not intend to show an astronomical system. He quotes an anonymous

---

[88] http://www.astronomy.ohio-state.edu/~pogge/Ast161/Unit3/response.html
[89] Jerome Langford, *Galileo, Science and the Church* (Ann Arbor: University of Michigan Press, 1992), 73.

ecclesiastical friend (scholars attribute this to a Cardinal Baronius): "the intention of the Holy Ghost is to teach us how one goes to heaven, not how heaven goes."[90]

In 1616 a decree against Copernicus was issued. Galileo was instructed not to "hold or defend" his model. In 1630 he published his "Dialogue Concerning the Two Chief World Systems," intended to be an imaginary conversation about the various options. He put arguments in favour of Aristotelian/Ptolemaic system in the mouth of a character named Simplicio (the fool), who spouted the current Pope's agnosticism about heavenly motion (due to the thesis that God can create any way he wants to and doesn't need to tell humans).

In 1633 Galileo was tried for disobeying the church's injunction not to teach what it had declared false. In the end, they did not execute Galileo, but instead ruled that his ideas were heretical and requested that he recant the opinions they considered false and dangerous. He agreed (after all, they could have tortured him). Galileo was forced to recant his support of the Copernican view that the earth moves around the sun, although legend has it that he muttered under his breath "yet it does move" after his sentence was read. He was sentenced to house arrest but since he was old and feeble that was not such an onerous assignment.

His reconciliation of the conflict relied on separating the interests of the two viewpoints. When reading Scripture, for example, he argued that
> in discussions of physical problems we ought to begin not from the authority of scriptural passages but from sense experiences and necessary demonstrations; for the holy Bible and the phenomena of nature proceed alike from the divine Word."[91]

---

[90] Galileo Galilei, "Letter to the Grand Duchess Christina" http://www.fordham.edu/halsall/mod/galileo-tuscany.html
[91] Ibid.

He accurately observed that the Bible rarely speaks of astronomical phenomena, and when it does (as in the case of the earth standing still for Joshua), it speaks in a way suited to the understanding of its readers. Galileo was not disturbed by the way that his scientific discoveries were presenting a new paradigm for thinking about the world because he simply saw his viewpoint as a different path towards truth.

Modern science established

The eternal mystery of the world is its comprehensibility.
Albert Einstein

As science continued to emerge in its own right, Christians were active in its development. The Galileo affair was not the final word because most scientific investigations simply did not have relevance to theological doctrine. Jesuit science was very fruitful: "Between 1600 and 1773, some 1,600 different Jesuits contributed nearly 6,000 original scientific works."[92] How were scientists (many of whom were also theologians) to think of their relation to God? The overall impetus of science was of theological import since it was a new way of thinking that proceeded independently. Science was a way of discovering the glory of God's creation.

John Dillenberger says: "The glory of seventeenth-century science belongs to England."[93] The Royal Society (with significant representation from Christians) was founded to further the discoveries of scientists. Richard Olson writes that, opposed to those who drew conclusions about the physical world from reason alone, "Other mechanical philosophies, such as those developed by Robert Boyle and Pierre Gassendi, were

---

[92] Richard Olson, *Science and Religion 1450-1900: From Copernicus to Darwin* (Greenwood Press, 2004), 69.
[93] John Dillenberger, *Protestant Thought and Natural Science* (Abingdon Press, 1960), 104.

grounded in experience, which could give only probable knowledge."[94] Experience is the most direct and immediate form of knowledge. However, it is particular and individual. Thus it must be checked against other experiences, and can never encompass all possible experiences.

Robert Boyle (1627-1691) "compared the physical world with clockwork in order to emphasize, not detract from, the sovereignty of God."[95] Boyle saw this knowledge contributing to theology: "The situation of the Celestial bodies afford not such strong arguments for the wisdom and design of God, as the bodies of animals and plants."[96] Thus, Boyle postulates that the world

> is like a rare clock, such as may be that at Strasbourg, where all things are so skillfully contrived, that the engine being once set a moving, all things proceed, according to the artificer's first design, and the motions of the little statues, that at such hours perform these or those things, do not require, like those of puppets, the peculiar interposing of the artificer, or any intelligent agent employed by him, but perform their functions upon particular occasions, by virtue of the general and primitive contrivance of the whole engine.[97]

God's design of the world was good, but sometimes the design seems not to take account of people (couldn't God have designed a world which is more hospitable?).

Rene Descartes (1596-1650), a mathematician and philosopher, viewed everything as 'matter in motion,' with no necessity for God to intervene. Descartes was enough of an idealist to work out a proof of God immediately after he affirmed his famous "*cogito ergo sum*" (I think, therefore I am). In this

---

[94] Olson, 73.
[95] John Hedley Brooke, *Science and Religion: Some Historical Perspectives* (Cambridge University Press, 1991), 160.
[96] Dillenberger, 115.
[97] Klaaren 155; from Boyle, *Notion of Nature IV*, 362.

respect, he was still relying on logic rather than experience as fundamental principles of thinking.

Blaise Pascal (1623-1662) was another mathematician and theologian. He argued that "experiments are the true teachers which one must follow in physics."[98] He took the results of science and concluded theologically that this finite world requires belief in God. Pascal recognized that there is a disproportion between God's reality and ours. First he looked at the nature of the universe and said:

> Let man contemplate Nature in its entirety, high and majestic; let him expand his gaze from the lowly objects which surround him. Let him look on this blazing light, placed like an eternal lamp in order to light up the universe; let him see that this earth is but a point compared to the vast circle which this star describes and let him marvel at the fact that this vast orbit itself is merely a tiny point compared to the stars which roll through the firmament.[99]

Then he goes beyond the visible, material realm: "Nature is an infinite sphere in which the center is everywhere, the circumference is nowhere. Finally, it is the greatest sensible mark of God's omnipotence, that our imagination loses itself in that thought."[100] His meditations on infinity are a prelude to a realization of God's transcendence breaking into our reality.

Pascal asked: "How could a part possibly know the whole?"[101] The very finiteness of our existence calls out for some infinite context. He emphasized that

> while reason might be able to establish that God exists, it could not establish any of the characteristics of an infinite divine being, just as it could not establish such

---

[98] http://authorscalendar.info/bpascal.htm, quoting Pascal, "Traités de l'équilibre des liqueurs et de la pesanteur de la masse de l'air."
[99] Pascal, *Pensées* (Penguin Books, 1966), 72.
[100] Ibid.
[101] Ibid., 92.

characteristics as the oddness or evenness of an infinite number. Only a direct, intuitive acceptance of God could guarantee belief, and such an acceptance was an issue for the heart, rather than for the head.[102]

When Pascal died, a paper was discovered sewn into the lining of his clothes, recording an experience he had. It fittingly describes his faith:

> The eve of Saint Chrysogonus martyr and others.
> From about half-past ten in the evening
> until about half-past midnight.
> Fire.
> The God of Abraham, the God of Isaac, the God of Jacob.
> Not of the philosophers and intellectuals.
> Certitude, certitude, feeling, joy, peace.
> The God of Jesus Christ.[103]

For Pascal, the primary motivation for religion came from the heart, but the intellect could give intimations of God's presence.

Newton and the deists

I do not know what I may appear to the world; but to myself I seem to have been only like a boy playing on the seashore, and diverting myself in now and then finding a smoother pebble or a prettier shell than ordinary, whilst the great ocean of truth lay all undiscovered before me.
Isaac Newton

Sir Isaac Newton (1643-1727), who pioneered some of the most significant scientific developments, was also a notable Biblical

---

[102] Olson, 79.
[103] Pascal (this fragment is not part of the text of *Pensées*, but was found sown into the lining of Pascal's coat after his death: see http://www.mathpages.com/home/kmath558/kmath558.htm).

scholar, and wrote interpretive commentaries on the books of Daniel and Revelation. His contributions to science are significant not so much because of any new discoveries, but rather by supplying imaginative theoretical approaches that explain long-observed events (such as the effects of gravity). Newton wrote that "this most beautiful system of the sun, planets and comets ... could only proceed from the counsel and dominion of an intelligent and powerful being,"[104] thus placing his scientific theories within his religious beliefs.

John Dillenberger argues that Newton focused on "the description of observable, mechanical, mathematical laws of nature."[105] However, theologically speaking, Newton could also add that God was everywhere in the universe, although we cannot see empirical evidence of this because God is not material. In the *General Scholium*, Newton defines it thus: "[God] endures forever, and is everywhere present; and, by existing always and everywhere, he constitutes duration and space." He goes on to argue that God is greater than creation, and is not affected by nature: "In him are all things contained and moved; yet neither affects the other: God suffers nothing from the motion of bodies; bodies find no resistance from the omnipresence of God."[106] Theology, then, is the study of the creator, while science studies the creation.

Newton was one of those scientists who placed science in the context of theology. John Hedley Brooke argues that Newton believed in "a God whose sovereign will had not only dictated the properties bestowed on matter, but was also capable of immediate action whether directly or indirectly through the

---

[104] Isaac Newton, *Principia*, quoted by Richard Westfall, "The Rise of Science and the Decline of Orthodox Christianity: A Study of Kepler, Descartes and Newton," in David Lindberg and Ronald Numbers, eds. *God and Nature* (University of California Press, 1986), 229.
[105] Dillenberger, 120.
[106] Isaac Newton, "General Scholium" from *Mathematical Principles of Natural Philosophy*. https://isaac-newton.org/general-scholium/

agency of natural causes."[107] Science can examine all of God's works, but not God, since God is not bound by our notions of existence. Newton thought that God's nature brings the universe into being. Hodgson argues that "Newton makes it clear that space is not absolute in itself but only as an emanative effect of God. Space and time are in no way part of God, but God's being implies infinite space and time."[108] Nature is not identical with God but it proceeds from God's being.

Newton was careful about speculating beyond the results of his observations. He says that "Gravity must be caused by an agent acting constantly according to certain laws, but whether this agent be material or immaterial I have left to the consideration of my readers."[109] He postulated that God holds the stars in place, otherwise they would collapse together (or at least that God created them so far apart that their gravitational affinity is next to zero).

As a theologian, Newton believed that "[t]he same mind that set up rules for interpreting nature did the same for the correct interpretation of scripture."[110] Scripture was thus amenable to rational interpretation, and would yield empirical results. He scoured the Scriptures for prophecies that would give evidence for the activity of God in history, especially in political affairs. He was looking for evidence, and fulfilled prophecies would satisfy a scientific mind that needs evidence from the senses.

Those who followed Newton (often called the deists) could take his clockwork universe and dispense with the clockmaker. Brooke argues:

> By speculating, for example, on the mechanism by which God reformed the solar system, he drew attention to the role of providence in nature—but at a price. Those

---

[107] Brooke, 136.
[108] Hodgson, 142.
[109] Brooke, 145.
[110] Ibid., 149.

who did not share his religious sensibilities would look at the mechanism and see no further.[111]

Note that this applies only to nature. God might not intervene in the physical actions of the cosmos, but the Bible witnesses to God's acts in history. The question is where (by miraculous means?) and when (with respect to whom?). Newton was convinced that God intervened in nature and history.

Newton's theoretical explanations of the motions of the planets introduced an important notion into our vocabulary, namely, inertia. His first law of motion, that an object in motion continues to move without any additional force, illustrates the new scientific thinking. The suggestion that the universe can go along its merry way without external intervention became the pattern of explanation favoured by natural philosophers.[112] This type of explanation of the world, it should be noted, is compatible with the Christian doctrine of providence, in which God continues to uphold and sustain creation, enabling the universe to continue to exist. However, the questions remain: Does God intervene in the natural history of the world (as in human history). Was creation a once-and-for-all event, or does God continually create? Does this happen in a way that contravenes natural laws, or has God instilled something of His creative energy in the laws themselves?

Pierre Laplace put it most succinctly when asked about the place of God's intervention in the universe. Legend has it that when Napoleon asked him about the absence of any mention of God in his *Celestial Mechanics*, Laplace said, "I had no need of that hypothesis."[113] Christians in the 18th century tended to answer him by saying that the universe had to start somehow, and God must be the only explanation for that beginning. This idea of God, ironically, applies the metaphor of scientist to God,

---

[111] Ibid., 145.
[112] This idea is developed in Wolfhart Pannenberg's *Toward a Theology of Nature: Essays on Science and Faith* (Westminster/J. Knox Press, 1993).
[113] http://scienceworld.wolfram.com/biography/Laplace.html

who starts an experiment, and then simply waits to see how it turns out. The God pictured in the Bible is considerably more active than that, intervening in the course of history. One of the most important interventions is the creation of life, especially human life, and the particular uniqueness of the human soul, destined for salvation in the great drama of the Christian view of history.

Biology: The God of life

I am inclined to look at everything as resulting from designed laws, with the details, whether good or bad, left to the working out of what we may call chance.
Charles Darwin

The Lord created human beings out of earth,
  and makes them return to it again.
He gave them a fixed number of days,
  but granted them authority over everything on the earth.
He endowed them with strength like his own,
  and made them in his own image.
Sirach 17:1-3

Humans have long been fascinated by the inner workings of living beings. We wonder at the spark of vital energy that sets life apart from its material context. What is this 'breath of God' that invigorates us and other animals, this "force that through the green fuse that drives the flower?"[114] However, in the last two hundred years, we have seen the rise of scientific theories that seek to explain life in wholly natural terms, without requiring the intervention of God. This contribution to our knowledge of life requires Christians to re-think God's relation to creation.

---

[114] Dylan Thomas, "The Force that Through the Green Fuse drives the Flower."

Charles Darwin's work began to unravel the theological rationales of creation seen as a perfect plan by a rational creator. His theories do not display a less complex universe (quite the opposite), but his descriptions of variations within species provide an explanation of how life could emerge through entirely natural processes. Darwin's key contribution was that these variations are set in the midst of a struggle for survival in the environment. This interaction produces change in the makeup of the species, even modifications that create new species. His sailing voyage on the H.M.S. *Beagle* allowed him to observe such variations in populations of animals and plants very close to each other, but separated by mountains or water, thus indicating a history of development of characteristics. When he published *The Origin of Species* in 1859 almost twenty-five years later, he was able to display copious evidence for the ability of life to adapt to its environment.

Darwin's theories force us to reconsider ourselves as the image of God. While Darwin titled his later work *The Descent of Man*, we can just as easily think of this process as an ascent towards God. Many Christians, however, on first considering the implications of evolution, were offended by the prospect of human beings developing from other animals. What aspect of the human being was a reflection of God? Surely not our animal nature! Further, the introduction of the element of chance in the process of the history of the world alters our conception of an intelligent designer. What sort of God would allow the world to proceed according to chance?

The theory of evolution seemed to provide a direct challenge to the Scriptural accounts of how the world came into being. Some tried to reconcile the Genesis accounts of the creation of the world and of human beings with the scientific story. The days of creation were interpreted as 'ages' in the development of the world (and the sequence is quite close to the scientific story, although some parts don't fit, such as the creation of the stars and sun on the fourth day). Others interpreted the Biblical story as a myth intended to proclaim the greatness of God, the ultimate source of the universe (and the details of how God created did not matter). Although the usual objections have been loudest in the Christian community, there have also been Muslim scholars who have voiced religious objections to evolutionary theory (although the Qur'an does not contain the specific details of what happened on each of the six days described in the Torah).

Some, however, clung to a literal interpretation of the creation story and attempted to find scientific support for a six-day creation. In a way, the creationists are trying to beat the scientists at their own game by arguing that creation is a better scientific explanation of the origins of life than evolution (for example, claiming that the dinosaur bones were buried in the earth by the flood described in Genesis). The burden of proof, though, seems to lie with the creationists, since the evidence is overwhelmingly in favour of evolution. Lately, the creationists have focused more on attacking the gaps in evolutionary theory, as well as emphasizing that evolution is 'just a theory.' The question, however, is which theory better explains the available, observable evidence.

Some theologians see the theory of evolution as prodding us to take seriously the role of freedom in the universe, not just in human life. Maybe God is waiting to be surprised about what direction evolution will take! Rather than dictating a grand design right from the beginning, God allows the future to be open-ended, which allows for the act of creation to be ongoing. This would mean that all that we see in the evolutionary process (even the seemingly negative parts) are a part of an overall divine design.

The most ambitious integrator of theology and evolution was the Jesuit Pierre Teilhard de Chardin. He observed the developing complexity of life through the evolutionary process, and saw God as the energy which drew the process towards fulfillment. He drew inspiration from the apostle Paul's vision of the reign of Christ: "to bring all things in heaven and on earth together under one head, even Christ" (Ephesians 1:10). De Chardin thought that the physical world was not forsaken by God, but has been "groaning as in the pains of childbirth" (Romans 8:23), waiting for Christ to redeem it. The suffering in the natural world thus has a significance (although it might not be seen as actually part of the divine plan).

The process of evolution can be seen as an involvement of God in the world. Josef Zycinski writes: "God, participating in a cosmic kenosis, draws to Himself an evolving world."[115] This perspective solves some of the problems involved in considering the suffering involved in the process. Jurgen Moltmann agrees:

> In the bondage of creation, in the pains of the body and in the yearning of believers, the Spirit is co-imprisoned and co-suffering, and keeps the waiting and the hoping alive through his own wordless and inexpresible sighs. We can surely understand this as meaning that God the Creator, who has entered into his creation through his Spirit, himself holds created being in life.[116]

God is in a sense involved in the creation of life through the endless process of variation and competition.

Some interesting developments today try to interpret evolutionary theory in a light more congenial to theology. Simon Conway Morris, for example, elucidates the ways in which evolution here on earth has developed similar trajectories in very different environments. He even claims that "convergences are

---

[115] Jozef Zycinski, *God and Evolution* (Catholic University of America Press, 2006), 5.
[116] Jurgen Moltmann, *God in Creation: A New Theology of Creation and the Spirit of God* (San Francisco: Harper and Row, 1985), 69.

global,"[117] such as animal numerosity (showing that the ability to count can develop independently in different species). This doesn't necessarily imply that there is a divine force driving the process, but it makes it easier for religious people to see a convergence between their faith and the scientific theory.

Origins

O God, great womb of wondrous love,
your Spirit moving on the deep
did wake a world within yourself,
a pulsing lighted world, from sleep.
...
O fire, O firmament and sea,
your seething ferment's energy
called forth a whirling waltz of life,
each plant and creature and its seed.
Harris J. Loewen

Many take the theory of evolution to be atheistic. John Haught, in his presentation of the conflict between evolution and creation, asks: "Why would we need to invoke the idea of God if chance and natural selection alone can account for all the creativity in the story of life?"[118] Richard Dawkins goes even further because the theory of evolution explains the process of life in purely natural terms without recourse to a supernatural cause, which allows him to be an "intellectually fulfilled atheist."[119]

However, theologians can still insist that God is the source of these laws, which allow the creation to develop in

---

[117] Simon Conway Morris, "Evolution and the Inevitability of Intelligent Life" in Peter Harrison, ed. *Cambridge Companion to Science and Religion* (Cambridge University Press, 2010), 151.
[118] John Haught, *Science and Religion: From Conflict to Conversation* (Paulist Press, 1995), 49.
[119] Richard Dawkins, *The Blind Watchmaker* (Penguin, 1991), 6.

freedom, producing novelty and complexity out of simpler forms. Kenneth Miller argues that "Mutations are a continuing and inexhaustible source of variation, and they provide the raw material that is shaped by natural selection."[120] This is a marvellous creation. It is true that it involves death and pain and suffering, but it also includes the urge of life to develop, to triumph over adversity, and even to cooperate in order to survive.

On the other side of the conflict, creationists argue that the Bible presents an explanation that is diametrically opposed to the scientific view. The creationists argue that either you have to believe in God or believe in evolution (and they use the word 'believe' for both in order to emphasize their view that the scientific account is a faith system rather than a proven theory). In contrast to this view, evolution is a different level of reasoning (science describes and explains the process of life, while religion explains its meaning). Theology interprets evolution and gives an explanation of the role of human beings in this story of the history of life arising in the universe.

Evolution is not a directed process. It produces a diversity of forms blindly, and it depends on the interaction with the environment to select the most fit for that niche. Keith Ward says: "The most efficient replicator might be something like a giant poisonous weed, or at least a number of such weeds in symbiotic competition, which kill off all incipiently more complex forms, strangling them before they can take root."[121] Biologists now talk about co-evolution: "The development of the individual cells of an organism is closely correlated with, and looks as though it is determined by, the needs of the whole organism."[122] The process of life is intimately connected with the

---

[120] Kenneth R. Miller, *Finding Darwin's God* (Cliff Street Books, 1999), 49.
[121] Keith Ward, *God, Chance and Necessity* (Oneworld: 1996), 135.
[122] Ibid., 135-6.

environment, so much that the environment in a sense determines the direction of evolution.

Evolution is blind but it contains within itself the possibility of producing complexity and diversity. Ward suggests that "bits of DNA would exist, not for their own sakes or simply to replicate themselves, but in order to build bodies which could at some stage contain consciousness, capable of apprehending and creating intrinsic values."[123] Our genes, in effect, contain the possibility for us to transcend our genetic heritage, and act independently of our 'animal' impulses. In this view, God created the world through the natural process of evolution. Life and death are natural processes that God used to develop complexity and novelty, thus giving nature freedom to develop. Nature thus has the capacity within itself to develop sentient beings such as humans, and God has chosen to breathe a soul into each one of us. This soul contains the freedom to do good or evil (consciousness and imagination give rise to choice between different behaviours).

An alternative tradition within the monotheistic tradition locates the changes of evolution in the kabbalistic tradition of Judaism. Geoffrey Cantor sees this process "within the larger framework provided by the Kabbalistic account of change. On this account all potentialities are imminent at the Creation and the universe unfolds progressively."[124] Rabbi Abraham Isaac Kook takes it a step further by relating the changes of evolution to their source in God: "By responding to illumination by the divine from above, all lower aspects of the world are drawn upward and eventually achieve perfection."[125] These mystical texts place biological development in the framework of a spiritual process.

---

[123] Ibid., 139.
[124] Geoffrey Cantor, "Modern Judaism," in Brooke and Numbers, *Science and Religion around the World*, 51.
[125] Ibid.

One can also see this pattern in the Qur'an: "We created man from a product of wet earth ... then fashioned we from the drop a clot ... then a little lump" (Qur'an 23: 12; I think the translation uses the royal 'we' although Muslims believe there is one God). The creation of man takes place in a process (developing from more primordial elements). This view may be related to the verse in Genesis 2 about Adam being fashioned out of the mud. Some Muslim commentators have attempted to compare verses like this in the Qur'an to modern embryology.

In Eastern religions, the development of life is more easily seen as a progression through stages. Vivekenanda relates this idea to a fundamental Hindu concept of the One which is the source of all multitude manifestations of reality: "Vedic protagonists traced all species back to a primordial "Supreme Being" from which everything had devolved."[126] Interestingly, this view sees everything developing into a less perfect form than the ultimate spiritual existence.

Pope John Paul II saw no necessary contradiction between the theory of evolution and Christian faith. He gives a good definition of the role of scientific theory: "A theory is a metascientific elaboration... A theory's validity depends on whether or not it can be verified, it is constantly tested against the facts."[127] Evolution as a theory is simply the best explanation of the data that we have in front of us. As such, it is subject to the usual scientific tests, and must survive as a paradigm in the scientific community, open to all challenges.

A purely naturalist account of human origins leaves something out, namely, the breath of God. The Pope disagreed with philosophical interpretations of the theory: specifically, those that "consider the mind as emerging from the forces of living matter, or as a mere epiphenomenon of this matter, are

---

[126] B. V. Subbarayappa, "Indic Religions" in Brooke and Numbers, *Science and Religion around the World*, 204.
[127] Pope John Paul II, "Magisterium is Concerned with Question of Evolution." http://www.cin.org/jp2evolu.html

incompatible with the truth about man. Nor are they able to ground the dignity of the person."[128] The soul cannot arise from natural causes. It is a rupture in the fabric of existence, making us into beings that are not purely material. This is not to say that something is added to the human being (some spiritual entity that can be measured). It is simply a statement about the ontological status of human beings, a statement that cannot be made about other material beings.

John Paul II accepted science as a reliable guide to obtaining knowledge about the natural world. He drew a line, though, between our theological beliefs about the origin of nature (that is, the creation of the entire universe of matter and life) and our study of nature (including our discovery of laws that describe the way that nature changes). That means that when we study nature, we are studying God's works (although we may not understand them fully).

Intelligent design

If life begins in carbon's dancing atoms
Moving in quadrilles of light
To the music of pure numbers,
Death is the stately measure
Of Time made plausible
By carbon's slow procession
Out of the shifting structure
Of crumbling flesh and bone.
A. M. Sullivan, "Atomic architecture"

Darwin's theory of evolution introduced a radically new way of looking at life. Instead of being created in unchanging forms, it develops into new configurations, which are selected for their

---

[128] Ibid.

fitness by the environment. This process seems to remove any need for God as an explanation.

Religious believers have often used the argument from design to defend their idea that God created the world. The classic exposition of the argument from design was by William Paley: If you find a watch lying on the beach, you will conclude that it could not have been formed by chance but must have been designed. In contrast, Dawkins says: "the only watchmaker in nature is the blind forces of physics, albeit deployed in a very special way."[129] He acknowledges that "Complicated things, everywhere, deserve a very special kind of explanation.... Biology is the study of complicated things that give the appearance of having been designed for a purpose."[130] But he stridently argues that the apparent design can be explained sufficiently by the natural laws that we see operating in the wonderful diversity of life.

The complicated interconnection is not purely random chance, as many opponents of evolution like to characterize it. Dawkins writes:

> Natural selection, the blind, unconscious, automatic process which Darwin discovered, and which we now know is the explanation for the existence and apparently purposeful form of all life, has no purpose in mind.[131]

It is a carefully balanced set of natural forces: the fecundity of life expressed in the incredible process of reproduction, the wisdom of death as it carefully winnows out those most fit to survive in a particular ecological niche, and the chance mutations or copying errors operating in our DNA.

Today, a new version of the argument from design has been proposed as a scientific research program (searching for examples of "intelligent design"). The proponents of intelligent

---

[129] Richard Dawkins, *The Blind Watchmaker* (Penguin, 1991), 5.
[130] Ibid., 1.
[131] Ibid., 5.

design argue that life shows us irreducibly complex forms that cannot have come about by the process of mutation and natural selection. The eye, for example, is composed of a collection of components that have to work together. If one is missing, the system cannot function. Michael Behe, for example, challenges "the idea that complex biological structures could possibly happen by means of gradual accretions of random mutations chosen and preserved by natural selection."[132] Therefore, a gradual process of accumulation of parts over long periods of time is not a sufficient explanation.

The age-old argument from design is thus introduced as a scientific hypothesis. William Dembski formulates this as a methodological shortcoming of biology: it does not even admit the possibility of 'intelligent design' (that is, complex structures that could not arise through natural processes, and thus require some intelligent designer, presumably). He draws from currently operating scientific research programs that search for signs of 'design' (such as cryptography). Dembski argues that "chance and necessity have proven insufficient to account for all scientific phenomena. Without invoking the rightly discarded teleologies, entelechies, and vitalisms of the past, one can still see that a third mode of explanation is required, namely, intelligent design."[133] All of these activities, he argues look for an ordered set of information that is distinguished by its complexity. He claims: "There now exists a rigorous criterion—complexity-specification—for distinguishing intelligently caused objects from unintelligently caused ones."[134] This criterion is similar to the algorithms for finding intelligent messages in radio waves from space.

Advocates of intelligent design suggest that it opens up the intellectual process. Dembski argues:

---

[132] David Neff, "The Pope, the Press and Evolution," *Christianity Today* (January 6, 1997). http://www.ctlibrary.com/1062
[133] William Dembski, "Science and Design," *First Things* (October 1, 1998).
[134] Ibid.

> Admitting design into science can only enrich the scientific enterprise. All the tried and true tools of science will remain intact.... Once we know that something is designed, we will want to know how it was produced, to what extent the design is optimal, and what is its purpose.[135]

Dembski is remarkably cautious about the identity of the designer implied by design. He is challenging scientists to reintroduce the notion of purpose into the discussion of physical things (something which scientists abhor, since it implies a conscious plan). Scientists prefer to talk about function rather than purpose, seeing the characteristics of things as simply parts of an overall system.

New versions of the argument of design suffer from the same defects they have always had (most adequately expressed in David Hume's *Dialogues on Natural Religion*). We cannot claim any inferences from viewing order in nature, since we have nothing to compare it with. We have no way of assigning probability to this order, because it is the only order that we see (and thus has probability of one, since it happened). It is just as likely to have happened by chance as by the intervention of God.

The argument from design is unconvincing to many. Natural disasters, the struggle for survival in nature, and the incredible pain that human beings can cause each other all count against the existence of an intelligent designer. The problem of evil is a profound challenge to any attempt to reconcile descriptions of the world with the idea of a God who made it. Christians usually explain this conundrum by appealing to the doctrine of sin, in which human beings refused the good gifts of God, and thus allowed evil into the world. This solution explains evil in human affairs, but the idea of sin does not apply to the natural world in the same way. Animals do not sin since they do not have free will. The effects of sin doubtlessly mar the natural

---

[135] Ibid.

creation, but surely they do not completely efface the goodness of God's original design.

Dawkins argues against irreducible complexity, that is, the idea that "complicated things have some quality, specifiable in advance, that is highly unlikely to have been acquired by random chance alone."[136] Biology, Dawkins suggests, acts as a method of explanation that uses a hierarchy of levels. He explains it thus: "For any given level of complex organization, satisfying explanations may normally be attained if we peel the hierarchy down one or two layers from our starting layer, but not more."[137] He calls this hierarchical reductionism: it "explains a complex entity at any particular level in the hierarchy of organizations, in terms of entities only one level down the hierarchy."[138] For the theist, God's creative activity shows the amazingly simple mechanisms by which an enormously complicated nature can be generated (by building the possibility for the emergence of life into the very structure of matter itself).

Various evolutionary theorists have attempted to construct plausible scenarios by which complex structures might have evolved. For example, Ursula Goodenough takes on the challenge to come up with an explanation for the bacterial flagellum (the tail-like appendage). She postulates a modification of the simple proto-cell that would be beneficial, but also produce a "collateral effect" that would pave the way for a flagellum to develop.[139] This kind of happy accident is not immediately beneficial, but allows other modifications that produce the more complex structure. Similar arguments have been advanced for the development of the eye, a very complex structure that is in fact present in nature in a multitude of forms

---

[136] Dawkins, 9.
[137] Ibid., 12.
[138] Ibid., 13.
[139] Ursula Goodenough, "The Mechanism of Evolution" in Matt Young, Taner Edis, eds. *Why Intelligent Design Fails* (Rutgers University Press, 2004), 68-9.

ranging from simple light-sensitive cells through eyes without focusing ability to the multi-functional human eye.

This is not to say that evolution has a direction, except towards a diversity of forms, some complex and some simple (whatever survives in an ecological niche, as long as that niche remains stable). Wentzel van Huyssteen acknowledges that "the process of evolution does not seem to be fine-tuned at all: evolutionary history can really seem random and makeshift."[140] However, we can notice that, at least in our experience of evolution, the tendency for complex things to develop is rather noticeable, especially in the development of thinking animals.

Our minds seem to beg for a religious explanation for our origins, not just a material process. Van Huyssteen sees the process of evolution itself as an accumulation of knowledge.[141] For example, DNA records information which is necessary for the development of cells, and this information is itself gradually modified by the evolutionary process. Ward posits that "the continuing causal activity of God seems the best explanation of the progress towards greater consciousness and intentionality."[142] The kind of complexity that we experience is the dramatic interconnectivity of the human brain, which allows us to be aware of our own evolutionary origins.

How did God design?

No creature has meaning
without the Word of God.
God's Word is in all creation, visible and invisible.
The Word is living, being,
spirit, all verdant greening,
all creativity.

---

[140] Wentzel van Huyssteen, *Duet or Duel? Theology and Science in a Postmodern World* (Trinity Press, 1998), 107.
[141] Ibid., 138.
[142] Ward, 178.

This Word flashes out in
every creature.
This is how the spirit is in
the flesh—the Word is indivisible from God.
Hildegard of Bingen

The intelligent design movement is an example of the "god-of-the-gaps" argument in which something we can't explain is used to suggest that God must have done it. Nature is seen as insufficient in itself to produce all of its marvels. Some magician has to pull a wand out and (presto!) zap some complex thing into existence. But isn't this a rather unintelligent way to run a world? Did the creator forget to include some ingredient in the recipe? Isn't it wiser on the part of God to build into nature its own recipe-making process, so that it can change itself as it goes along? Michael Denton makes a comprehensive argument that the "the laws of nature are uniquely prefabricated for life as it exists on earth"[143] but that biological structures show "genuine autonomous creativity so that the world of life might reflect in a mirror in some small measure the creativity of God."[144] Of course, nature is blind and the recipe changes only by random variations (introduced through the combinations achieved through sexual reproduction).

This process can be seen as the genius of God's design. It proceeds by small steps because that is the best way to survive in a changing environment. Adaptation is the key because nature doesn't know what's coming next. It has to produce all kinds of possibilities so that something will be there to deal with the unexpected. Richard Fern argues that "Creation is an act in progress, a product whose reality is not only present but yet to

---

[143] Michael Denton, *Nature's Destiny: How the Laws of Biology Reveal Purpose in the Universe.* (Free Press, 1998), xix.
[144] Ibid., 365.

come."[145] The laws of evolution may be governed by a nonlinear relationship: it could go in any direction, but there are patterns of stability. Eventually this gives rise to consciousness, in our case (the ascent of man, as Darwin could have called it). Many will object to the seemingly unintelligent design in this chaotic progression towards what seems so special to us. As Darwin was careful to point out, there is no steady progress in evolution towards a pre-designed outcome. It is more like a branching tree, diverging in all possible directions, scoping out the landscape (or design space, as it is sometimes called).

In the natural world we also see great suffering. Are we to think that God designed the world so that such things would happen? Pain and death surround us. Christian theology responds by saying that evil has no primary existence, but is a distortion of the goodness of God's creation. Does this mean that God intended a better world than we see? This is how most Christians read the first few chapters of Genesis: the story shows how our freedom brought sin and suffering into the world.

The creation of freedom seems to require a universe that is open to the possibility of things going wrong. Other religions see freedom as the cause of our grief! Michael Chapman argues that

> The Buddhist doctrine that human suffering derives from our cravings dovetails nicely with evolutionary psychology. Like apes and monkeys, for example, humans crave sweets to the dietary ruin of millions in today's 'supersized' world.[146]

This view places the mechanism of evolution in a natural framework but shows that everything that is created is not always good.

---

[145] Richard Fern, *Nature, God and Humanity: Envisioning an Ethics of Nature* (Cambridge University Press, 2002), 145.
[146] Michael Chapman, "Hominid Failings" in Philip Clayton and Jeffrey Schloss, eds. *Evolution and Ethics: Human Morality in Biological and Religious Perspective* (Grand Rapids, Mich.: W.B. Eerdmans Pub., 2004), 101.

Some theologians argue that there is great wisdom in the design built into the process of evolution. Keith Ward argues that the "formation of self-replicating molecules from complex combinations of chemical elements"[147] can be explained just as well by natural laws as by God's intervention. When these molecules arise, natural selection takes over. Changes in these molecules can produce positive effects: "The overall process of mutation, however, is clearly adaptive, when taken, as it should be, in its total causal environment."[148] Although it sounds cruel, adaptation has a progressive function ("no pain; no gain").

Instead of creating a static world that cannot change and develop, God built into the natural world the ability to adapt to changing conditions. Evolution is driven, in fact, by the constant process of organisms changing in minute ways (because of the marvellous process of reproduction, especially the development of new organisms by combining of the DNA of their parents). This capacity to change has allowed life to flourish in a multitude of ecological contexts (for example, through climactic changes like ice ages and the variety of conditions caused by the structure of the earth's crust, including continental drift and volcanic eruptions).

The process of evolution seems cruel, it is true. Death drives the process by weeding out the organisms less fit to survive. Nature, we are learning, encourages cooperative strategies to succeed in complicated ecosystems (symbiotic relationships all the way from fish cleaning the mouths of sharks to the complex interplay of the food chain). Some argue that it could only be this way if God chose to create a world with the capacity to produce human beings with conscious freedom.

It looks like the laws of evolution have allowed human beings to develop their particular brain capacity and social relationships. Our future has not been dictated by a God that

---

[147] Ward, 116.
[148] Ibid., 128.

programmed a computer game with only a few possible options. God devised a creation that has within itself the laws of mutation and development, with all of the mayhem that can develop within those constraints. Norris Clarke puts it this way:

> Such a creator must be a kind of daring Cosmic Gambler who loves to work with both law and chance, a synthesis of apparent opposites - of power and gentleness, a lover of both law and order and of challenge and spontaneity.[149]

Many religious people believe that God is ultimately in control of this creation, and eager to relate to all creatures, but especially those that have the cognitive capacity to be aware of their own possibility of relating to the source of life.

Creating good

Oh yet we trust that somehow good
  Will be the final goal of ill,
  To pangs of nature, sins of will,
Defects of doubt, and taints of blood;

That nothing walks with aimless feet;
  That not one life shall be destroy'd,
  Or cast as rubbish to the void,
When God hath made the pile complete;

That not a worm is cloven in vain;
  That not a moth with vain desire
  Is shrivell'd in a fruitless fire,
Or but subserves another's gain.

---

[149] W. Norris Clarke, "Is a Natural Theology Still Possible Today?" in Russell et al., ed., *Physics, Philosophy, and Theology,* 121 quoted by Elizabeth A. Johnson. "Does God Play Dice? Divine Providence and Chance." *Theological Studies*. 57.1 (Mar. 1996).

Behold, we know not anything;
  I can but trust that good shall fall
  At last–far off–at last, to all,
And every winter change to spring.
So runs my dream: but what am I?
  An infant crying in the night:
  An infant crying for the light:
And with no language but a cry.
Alfred, Lord Tennyson, "In Memoriam A.H.H" (LIV)

Genesis says that God made the world "very good." The natural laws bring about a marvelous diversity. This world is full of complex forms yet these forms are explainable by simple natural laws. Kenneth Miller recounts the following analogy given in a graduate seminar he attended:

> If you deny evolution, then the sort of God you have in mind is a bit like a pool player who can sink fifteen balls in a row, but only by taking fifteen separate shots. My God plays the game a little differently. He walks up to the table, takes just one shot, and sinks all the balls. I ask you which pool player, which God, is more worthy of praise and worship?[150]

The universe as we know it unfolds throughout time, and we are here to observe it and reflect upon it (the natural laws may have unfolded in entirely different ways since they contain within themselves an element of chance). Evolution contains within itself emergent properties (new forms can arise out of old; many possibilities exist). This is not a direction but many ends (for example, life tending towards consciousness—not necessarily human).

The laws are neutral (that is, they do not prove that God designed them) so that we would have freedom to choose God. If nature pointed directly to God there would be no need for faith.

---

[150] Miller, 283-4.

The laws are also morally neutral (evolution is not cruel, just blind—yes, there is lots of death and pain and suffering, but that is nature). Josef Zycinski claims: "The immanent God does not turn the dance of life into a romantic idyll. He expresses, however, his solidarity with man by the bond of participation in evolutionary meanderings bearing the mark of drama." [151] If matter itself is free to develop according to the statistical uncertainties of quantum theory (even if those are completely determined by variables as yet hidden to us), then there is an openness to the cosmos that is both good and bad. It allows possibilities unforeseen by us to develop (although it is still possible to conceive of God putting all of those possibilities in the mix).

Evolutionary theory need not rule out the idea of creation since this doctrine affirms not only that the universe is made by God but also that it depends on God for its continued existence. In this way, we can see God intimately involved in each moment and each place, constantly carrying the present world into the future. Keith Ward puts it this way: "the apparently random element is in fact the best way of achieving a goal-directed outcome, while leaving the process itself non-deterministic. Thus, a space is left for the free actions of intelligent beings."[152] The 'freedom' exhibited by DNA is simply an open future not determined by what has gone on in the past (not a conscious freedom to change).

Nature has the capacity within itself to develop sentient beings such as humans. Life developed in an amazing variety of directions, branching out to explore the many variations that can survive in the constantly changing environment of planet Earth. Diarmid O'Murchu argues that

---

[151] Joseph Zycinski, *God and Evolution*, (Catholic University of America Press, 2006), 181-2, 194.
[152] Ward, 93.

> The inherent capacity for self-organization in no way diminishes or undermines the notion of God's involvement in evolution's great story. ... We are abandoning the idea of an outside manipulator (engineer) in favor of an animating force from within, not because it gives us humans more power, but because the evidence of evolution requires us to make that adjustment.[153]

God's experiment of creation relies on chance and mutation to give life a certain amount of freedom and even creativity.

Death is intimately involved in this process of creation. Some organisms are not well-adapted (and many mutations or variations die). Pain and suffering and disease are part and parcel of the condition of life. Ward likens this to the basic physical processes of the universe: "If one is to have emergence in the universe, one has to have change and death, the elimination of old properties to make way for new. Out of the decay of nuclear particles, atomic structures are built."[154] This is simply the condition of life. It is the stage on which the human drama is played out.

The human story

From the greatness and beauty of created things comes a corresponding perception of their Creator.
Wisdom of Solomon 13: 5

The creation story in Genesis culminates with the creation of man. Many Christians feel that God has a divine plan set out for the cosmos, including the finest details of their lives. After all, Psalm 139 says:

---

[153] Diarmid O'Murchu, *Evolutionary Faith* (Orbis Books, 2002), 51.
[154] Ward, 192.

> I praise you because I am fearfully and wonderfully made;
>> your works are wonderful,
>> I know that full well.
> My frame was not hidden from you
>> when I was made in the secret place.
>> When I was woven together in the depths of the earth,
> your eyes saw my unformed body.
>> All the days ordained for me
>> were written in your book
>> before one of them came to be.
>> (Psalm 139: 14-16).

The overall sweep of the Christian story, from creation through redemption, is dependent on the mythical framework that is established through the narrative of the first few chapters of Genesis. The opening act sets the stage for the great drama to follow: the rescue of humankind from their primordial error of turning away from God. This mythic framework explains the presence of evil in the world. Richard Coleman interprets the Genesis story more creatively to include this vision of human being: "Adam and Eve could be the first hominid group to evolve to the point where humans were sufficiently self-conscious to know they were created and responsible for their actions."[155] Evolution disrupts that neat and tidy explanation by noting the nasty elements built into the structure of matter itself and the way that they percolate up into the biological, social and psychological structures of human existence.

Other religions have myths of origins which also explain the origin of evil. One Buddhist creation myth goes like this:

---

[155] Richard Coleman, *State of Affairs: The Science-Theology Controversy* (Lutterworth Press, 2015), 14.

> When a cosmos comes to an end and contracts, and before a new cosmos begins, beings are mostly born in the Abhassara Brahma world.
>
> These luminous beings live for a long time, feeding on nothing but delight. And while the cosmos has contracted, there are no suns or stars, planets or moons.
>
> In the last contraction, in time an earth formed, beautiful and fragrant and sweet to taste. Beings who tasted the earth began to crave it. They sat gorging themselves on the sweet earth, and their luminescence disappeared. The light that left their bodies became the moon and sun, and in this way night and day were distinguished, and months, and years, and seasons.
>
> As the beings stuffed themselves with sweet earth, their bodies became courser. Some of them were handsome, but others were ugly. The handsome ones despised the ugly ones, and became arrogant, and as a result the sweet earth disappeared. And they were all very sorry.[156]

This story of the creation of the universe has parallels to the Christian story of the fall of human beings. The impeccably ordered goodness of creation is marred by the ungrateful rejection of the gift, and so humankind is banished from the orderly circle of the good creation. The primary gift given to humans is that of freedom. We have been given the ability to rationally examine creation. We cannot create anything totally new (something *ex nihilo*, that is, something not inherent in the capacity of creation itself) but we can put it together in ways different than are immediately apparent.

---

[156] "The Agganna Sutta (A Buddhist Creation Fable)"
http://buddhism.about.com/od/thetripitaka/a/The-Agganna-Sutta.htm

Are we alone in the cosmos or are we put here by a higher power? That is the question that creation myths attempt to answer. Why is there so much evil and suffering in the world? If you believe in a good God, that is a terribly difficult question. The theory of evolution is not antithetical to this picture. It does require us to re-conceptualize God's role in the ongoing development of the universe. God creates things that grow, that are tested, that change in order to become more than they were before. Life emerges from lower levels through simple processes that have the possibility of complexity built within them. It allows us to participate in bringing the universe into actual existence (for good or evil). Ironically, the theory of evolution is seen by creationists as the source of many of the evils they currently perceive in the Western world. However, we will see that the theory of evolution can actually explain the development of moral behaviour in animals as well as human beings.

Physics: matter matters

When the Lord created his works from the beginning,
  and, in making them, determined their boundaries,
he arranged his works in an eternal order,
  and their dominion for all generations.
They neither hunger nor grow weary,
  and they do not abandon their tasks.
They do not crowd one another,
  and they never disobey his word.
Sirach 16:26-28

If atoms are mostly empty space then why is matter so solid? The physicist's view of the world as expressed in their complicated theories challenges our common-sense understanding of the world. But does it matter what things are made of? As Shakespeare wrote in *Romeo and Juliet*, "A rose by any other name would smell as sweet." Our ordinary existence is still understood in terms of air and water, earth and fire (especially for those who live close to the land). But where did this all come from? Religious believers can still profess that God made the world, right down to the smallest quark and meson. However, new scientific pictures of the world force us to re-examine our ideas about God's relation to the world.

These theories are difficult to understand and have sometimes been misinterpreted by the general public (including theologians). Part of the difficulty arises because scientists rely on instruments that observe the effects of the elementary particles rather than the particles themselves (they are too small for us to see, even with the aid of the best instruments). Heisenberg's uncertainty principle has the effect of undermining the objectivity of science. According to him, the most fundamental particles cannot be observed with complete certainty: the more accurately one tries to measure the velocity of an elementary particle, the less accurately its position can be measured (and vice versa).

According to one interpretation of this theory, the act of observing the most fundamental particles of the universe affects their actions. However, scientists disagree about the interpretation of some of these theories. Einstein, for example, disliked the explanations of quantum theory because they describe the behaviour of atomic particles within a range of probabilities. This led to his famous comment that "God does not play dice with the universe."[157] He wanted a theory which could identify the location of electrons with perfect precision. Notice that this displays a particular view of God, namely that God requires rigid order and would not want any elements of uncertainty in the universe.

More and more, physicists are seeing that matter and energy interact in a complex dance at the basis of our material existence. Einstein showed that matter could be converted into energy with his famous equation ($E=mc^2$). Later, scientists began to apply the models of energy to matter, and vice versa. Light, for example, can be described both as a wave and as a particle. Similarly, with the advent of quantum theory, scientists began to see an elementary particle as a complex wave-pattern, since this structure seemed to explain the behaviour of the atom.

---

[157] https://www.goodreads.com/work/quotes/326504-the-born-einstein-letters

Theories of physics also act as models by which to think about the relation of theology and science. The wave-particle model of light, for example, in which a fundamental reality of our universe can be interpreted and even described in two equally satisfactory ways, is used by many theologians to explain how theology and science can both describe the same world. This model is particularly attractive since we need both models in order to explain all of the actions of light. Applying the model to the relation between science and theology allows each explanation of the world its own independence, but requires them to be in dialogue in order to fully understand the world.

Beginnings and endings

If the universe is really completely self-contained, having no boundary or edge, it would have neither beginning nor end, it would simply be. What place, then, for a creator?
Stephen Hawking

Where did it all come from? By looking out into the universe, scientists see a vast array of emptiness, dotted occasionally with unimaginably dense stars and dark clouds of matter left over from the formation of planets and suns. All of these majestic objects are receding from us as the universe expands. Does the universe have a boundary, an edge? It would be more accurate to say that space itself is expanding (but into what?). If it is expanding, does that mean it all started out in one tiny, timeless point?

Christians see the beginning of the universe through the lens of the metaphor of creation. Dietrich Bonhoeffer puts it this way:

> The Bible begins in a place where our thinking is at its most passionate. Like huge breakers it surges up, is thrown back upon itself and spends its strength. ... That

> the Bible should speak of the beginning provokes the world and irritates us. For we cannot speak of the beginning; where the beginning begins our thinking stops, it comes to an end. And yet the fact that we ask about the beginning is the innermost impulse of our thinking; for in the last resort it is this that gives validity to every true question we ask. We know that we must not cease to ask about the beginning though we know that we can never ask about it.[158]

Scientists try their hardest to answer these questions, although they are not subject to the usual pattern of investigation. We cannot do any repeatable experiments on the beginning of the universe, and so the observations we make have to be extrapolated back to that hypothetical beginning. Theories about the beginning of the universe are fueled by the development of telescopes that allow us to see further and further into space. Tools like the large hadron collider allow us to discover more elementary particles. Discoveries of objects like black holes enable us to understand the nature of the universe, and how it could have been formed.

The question of God remains a difficult one for physicists, because they would rather be able to explain the origins of the universe without having to fall back on a supernatural explanation. From a religious perspective, the idea of a Big Bang seems very attractive, since it seems to mesh with the idea of God bringing the world into being at one specific time. However, monotheistic religions would maintain that it is more important to emphasize that God created the world and that the world continues to depend on God for its existence. We should be wary of tying our belief about creation to any specific scientific theory, because it could change as we discover more about the universe.

---

[158] Dietrich Bonhoeffer, *Creation and Fall; Temptation* (London: SCM Press, 1959), 13.

Scientists today seem to agree with a version of Augustine's notion of time: the great theologian thought that there was "no 'before' since time came into being along with the rest of creation."[159] Stephen Hawking claims that "the universe has a finite age but no datable moment of origination."[160] We simply cannot identify a point in time when it began. Paul Davies notes that "Although Hawking's proposal is for a universe without a definite origin in time, it is also true to say in this theory that the universe has not always existed."[161] The laws of physics (including time as we know it) came into being in the process of the Big Bang. Don Page puts it this way:

> [T]his imaginary time had no beginning, it had no edge. It didn't necessarily go on forever. It was finite, just in the same way that there's only a finite amount of area in the earth, which doesn't go on forever as you go north—in some sense it comes to an end, since there is a farthest north you can go. But in another sense there's no real end there.[162]

The real question about the Big Bang is not whether it had a beginning, but whether it had a cause. It is not a question of temporal origin, but ontological. Davies says: "In modern scientific cosmology, one should no longer think of space-time as 'coming into existence' anyway. Rather, one says that space-time (or the universe) simply *is*."[163] Here's the rub: if the universe simply exists according to these natural laws, why would we posit a cause beyond the universe? It seems that the universe simply contains the laws to bring itself into being.

---

[159] John Polkinghorne, "Beyond the Big Bang," in Fraser Watts, ed. *Science Meets Faith* (London: SPCK, 1998), 17.
[160] Ibid., 17-18.
[161] Paul Davies, *The Mind of God* (Simon and Schuster, 1992), 68.
[162] Stephen Hawking, *Stephen Hawking's* A Brief History of Time: *A Reader's Companion* (Bantam Books, 1992), 136-7.
[163] Davies, *The Mind of God*, 69.

At one point, Hawking suggested that it is not enough for the laws to exist. He put it very poetically:
> Even if there is only one possible unified theory, it is just a set of rules and equations. What is it that breathes fire into the equations and makes a universe for them to describe? The usual approach of science of constructing a mathematical model cannot answer the questions of why there should be a universe for the model to describe. Why does the universe go to all the bother of existing?[164]

More recently, he has argued that the laws can exist by themselves: "Before we understand science, it is natural to believe that God created the universe. But now science offers a more convincing explanation."[165] Do mathematical laws have an inner necessity that brings about the material configurations that they describe?

There is a huge gap between our knowledge of the world and God's creative activity. Bonhoeffer argues that God's being transcends our reality of cause and effect. He says it passionately and poetically:
> Creator and creature cannot be said to have a relation of cause and effect, for between Creator and creature there is neither a law of motive nor a law of effect nor anything else. Between Creator and creature there is simply nothing: the void. For freedom happens in and through the void. There is no necessity that can be shown in God which can or must ensue in creation.[166]

Even our concepts of cause and effect are ways of dividing up the reality that we experience, and cannot be univocally applied to God's bringing the world into being.

---

[164] Stephen W. Hawking, *A Brief History of Time: From the Big Bang to Black Holes* (Bantam Books, 1988), 174.
[165] https://www.cnet.com/news/stephen-hawking-makes-it-clear-there-is-no-god/
[166] Bonhoeffer, 18.

In the Christian view, God brings the world into being through the internal relationships within the Godhead. The creative activity of the Father is paralleled by that of the Son (the Word that was with God in the beginning) and that of the Spirit (the Wisdom that also formed things). We use personal metaphors to describe the relationships between these creative actors because those are the most appropriate: God creates through a process of relating (loving the world into being). In Christian theology there is a sharp distinction between the creator and creation, which Bonhoeffer expresses as a void. We are finite but God is infinite and so our words describe God's being accurately but inadequately.

The anthropic principle

However successful our scientific explanations may be, they always have certain starting assumptions built in. ... one can ask where these laws come from in the first place.
Paul Davies

Life depends on a complex relationship between various physical constraints. For example, because water floats when it freezes, ice forms a skin on bodies of water rather than freezing all the way through (and thus destroying all sorts of life in the process). Other physical constraints which operate in the universe lead some to claim that this finely-tuned cosmos cannot be the result of a string of unlikely coincidences. Owen Gingerich defines this principle as follows: "the universe simply must be this way, as otherwise we wouldn't be alive to observe it."[167] This is the so-called "weak anthropic principle" (WAP). It seems to reduce to a tautology: "we're here because we're here because we're here." A stronger version argues that "even a small change in the

---

[167] Owen Gingerich, "Ingredients for Life," in Stannard, 19-20.

physical constants would have resulted in an uninhabitable universe."[168] In other words, it seems improbable that this incredible artifact could have just happened on its own.

The weak version of this principle simply states the obvious: if the universe were any different we wouldn't be here to observe it. We can imagine a universe forming with different physical properties, leading to complex configurations of life based on other chemical and environmental systems. The existence of complex pattern does not necessarily prove the existence of an intelligent designer. Although we probably do not know all of the factors contributing to structures arising in the world, it seems that we can satisfactorily explain them without invoking the aid of an intelligent cause.

Gingerich argues that the universe has its constants finely tuned to support life. He suggests that the universe looks like it is uniquely designed (in terms of its physical structure naturally coming together in the forms that we see, even the consciousness required to observe it). He sees evolution as the creation of a God intelligent enough to develop a process that, left to its own devices, comes up with the remarkable diversity of life that we see.[169] John Polkinghorne puts another twist on this:

> Maybe there is only one universe which is the way it is, in its finely-tuned anthropic fruitfulness, because it is not any old world but rather a creation endowed by its Creator with precisely the physical fabric that will enable it to fulfil the divine purpose of a fruitful evolutionary history.[170]

It seems like we could criticize him on the principle that "hindsight is 20/20" since he is suggesting that the idea of God presupposes the kind of universe that we in fact inhabit.

---

[168] Ian Barbour, *Religion and Science: Historical and Contemporary Issues* (HarperCollins, 1997), 204.
[169] Owen Gingerich, *God's Universe* (The Belknap Press of Harvard University Press, 2006).
[170] Polkinghorne, "Beyond the Big Bang," 21.

Time and time again, physicists have developed mathematical formulations for their theories which have suggested physical features of the universe as yet undiscovered, only to find them years later. Paul Davies remarks that "there must be an unchanging rational ground in which the logical, orderly nature of the universe is rooted."[171] He encapsulates the best form of the argument from design:

> The new physics and the new cosmology hold out a tantalizing promise: that we might be able to explain how all the physical structures in the universe have come to exist, automatically, as a result of natural processes. We should then no longer have need for a Creator in the traditional sense. Nevertheless, though science may explain the world, we still have to explain science. The laws which enable the universe to come into being spontaneously seem themselves to be the product of exceedingly ingenious design.[172]

This Platonic conception of the ideal structures of rationality becoming materialized in physical form doubtlessly comes from Davies' fascination with mathematics. However, the order of discovery does not imply ontological status. If the mathematical descriptions are simply representations of reality, this would explain why new descriptions are possible. He says: "Only the system *as a whole* gives concrete expression to microscopic reality."[173] The whole complement of reality must be seen as a system of relationships (leading to a tremendous complexity presumably describable in many different consistent ways).

The anthropic principle does not give any concrete conclusions about what kind of God creates a world like ours. Paul Davies writes:

---

[171] Davies, "What Happened before the Big Bang?" in Russell Stannard, *God for the 21st Century* (Templeton Foundation Press, 2000), 12.
[172] Paul Davies, *Superforce: The Search for a Grand Unified Theory of Nature* (Heinemann, 1984), 243.
[173] Ibid., 39.

> Through my scientific work I have come to believe more and more strongly that the physical universe is put together with an ingenuity so astonishing that I cannot accept it merely as a brute fact. There must, it seems to me, be a deeper level of explanation.[174]

He proposes that the evidence in front of us leads us to the idea of God. Davies goes on to say: "Whether one wishes to call that deeper level 'God' is a matter of taste and definition."[175] It isn't definitively the Christian God—it could just as easily be a non-personal force such as Buddhists conceive.

From a theological perspective, the underlying rational ground of emergence can be seen as God's work. Gordon D. Kaufman suggests that

> creativity (God)—the coming into being of the new, the emergence of the novel—seems to be happening virtually everywhere we look: from the Big Bang through the cosmic expansion into galaxies in which stars and planets emerge, through the appearance of life on planet Earth (and possibly elsewhere) and its evolution into countless forms, ultimately including human beings.[176]

This impersonal concept of creativity in nature is a long way from the personal concept of God in the monotheistic religions. It is closer to the idea of a spirit pervading the universe seen in Eastern religious views.

A purely physical explanation of the origin of the universe leaves us with the question: Where do the natural laws that bring the universe into existence come from? Paul Davies states the problem:

> It is still not clear that science could in principle explain everything in the physical universe. There remains that

---

[174] Davies, *The Mind of God*, 16.
[175] Ibid.
[176] Gordon D. Kaufman. "A Religious Interpretation of Emergence: Creativity as God." *Zygon: Journal of Religion & Science*. December 1, 2007.

> old problem about the end of the explanatory chain. ....
> Sooner or later we all have to accept something as given,
> whether it is God, or logic, or a set of laws, or some
> other foundation for existence. Thus, 'ultimate'
> questions will always lie beyond the scope of empirical
> science as it is usually defined.[177]

The problem with the anthropic principle lies in its tunnel vision. We do not observe any other universe and so we have nothing with which to compare ours. So the anthropic principle doesn't really prove anything since we only observe the values of our universe.

Uncertainty or indeterminacy?

Can nature possibly be as absurd as it seemed to us in these atomic experiments?
Werner Heisenberg

There is no quantum world. There is only abstract quantum physical description. It is wrong to think that the task of physics is to find out how nature is. Physics is concerned with what we can say about nature.
Neils Bohr

One of the most unexpected results of the new physics has been the realization that the fundamental bases of our existence are not as certain and immutable as was once thought. This realization began to dawn on physicists when Einstein introduced his theory of relativity. The nature of time was brought into question since the theory contradicts our notion that time marches on at equal speeds everywhere.

Einstein's theory of relativity is often thought to support purely subjective views of the universe. Sometimes my students

---

[177] Davies, *The Mind of God*, 15.

complain about their marks by saying: "It's all relative!" However, his theory could more properly be called a theory of invariance, for the laws of physics are the same in all frames of reference. An individual's perception of events may differ from someone in another frame of reference, but they are using the same tools to measure reality. It is true that in Einstein's theory there is no absolute frame of reference, but this should imply that we must constantly check our observations against others. The theory of relativity means that we have to factor our vantage point into the observation, but the information can be translated without loss of truth into another person's frame of reference.

The theory of relativity indicates that everything is related and that every perspective is equally valid because there is a mathematical relationship between them; one can translate from one to the other. It does not mean that there are no absolutes, since the laws of physics are the same for any observer, and we are all observing the same thing. John Gribbin explains it in this way:

> [A]ll observers moving at constant velocity relative to each other are equally entitled to regard themselves at rest, with every other observer in motion. It explains how moving clocks run slow (because time itself is slowed by motion), moving rulers shrink, and moving objects gain mass, compared to such a stationary observer.[178]

Einstein pictures the universe, then, in four dimensions: "although time and length are both distorted by motion, there is an underlying 'four-dimensional length' which stays the same."[179] This is called "space-time," and it finds expression not only in science fiction but also in the Big Bang theory of the universe expanding from a tiny point.

---

[178] John Gribbin, *Unveiling the Edge of Time* (Crown Publishers, 1992), 24.
[179] Ibid., figure 9 caption, 42.

Einstein's theory of relativity forced us to think differently about space and time but other developments in physics forced us to acknowledge that reality is not as predictable as we thought. Quantum theory revised our understanding of the smallest elements of the universe. Werner Heisenberg said: "you can't know where an atom, or electron, or whatever, is located and know how it is moving, at one and the same time."[180] Physicists disagreed about the interpretation of this model. Neils Bohr thought that uncertainty was part and parcel of the universe. In other words, "atomic uncertainty is truly intrinsic to nature."[181] On the other side, Einstein thought that "God does not play dice." Uncertainty is our problem; if we had complete knowledge, we could predict anything (eg. weather or stock market). Bohr proposed that the two models are complementary, since they can be easily converted one into the other, and can be used interchangeably. Peter Hodgson claims:

> We can only calculate the statistical properties of these systems, such as the half-life of radioactive decay or the differential scattering cross-section that the gives the probabilities that a particle is scattered through various angles. All measurements of quantum systems are of this statistical character.[182]

The equations give probability distributions for the behaviour of these entities rather than complete knowledge of the situation.

The standard interpretation, called the Copenhagen interpretation after the workplace of Neils Bohr, is that "a unique role was being played by classical measuring apparatus."[183] Yet other physicists, such as David Bohm, argue that "probabilities arise simply from ignorance of certain details."[184] He thought

---

[180] Davies, *God and the New Physics*, 102.
[181] Ibid.
[182] Peter Hodgson, *Theology and Modern Physics* (Ashgate, 2005), 145.
[183] John Polkinghorne, *Quantum Theory: A Very Short Introduction* (Oxford University Press, 2002), 48.
[184] Ibid., 53.

that hidden variables render the quantum events completely predictable and deterministic. We just don't understand how it works (yet)! Maybe the variables will someday be found.

Quantum mechanics is sometimes used to give support to the view that we create the reality that we observe. In Schrodinger's famous parable of the cat in a box, a quantum event gives rise to two different possibilities (the cat is alive or dead) but the actual state of affairs is not resolved until an observation is made (maybe if cats have nine lives it could be both at the same time!). Heisenberg thought that reality was actually indeterminate (it cannot be determined because it has no actual structure, only multiple possibilities, some of which get actualized). Niels Bohr thought that this gives a limit to our knowledge, stating that we cannot know both the mass and the momentum of a particle at the same time (note that this knowledge can be gained over successive time periods, which makes possible accurate predictions of the motion of the quanta). The quantum level is mysterious, but it obeys perfectly regular statistical laws.

Physicists refer to the "collapse of the wave-function," in which the observer affects reality by interacting with it (producing a determinate result). According to the Copenhagen interpretation, quanta exist in 'superposition,' that is, a multitude of possibilities at the same time. At the point of observation, however, one of those possibilities is realized. The famous controversies over quantum theory lie in how to interpret this result. Is there some hidden variable governing this result? Neils Bohr thought that "the fuzzy and nebulous world of the atom only sharpens into concrete reality when an observation is made. In the absence of an observation, the atom is a ghost."[185] John Wheeler thought that "The precise nature of reality … has to await the participation of a conscious observer. In this way, mind can be made responsible for the retroactive creation of

---

[185] Davies, 103.

reality."[186] Davies states that "the new physics has given 'the observer' a central role in the nature of physical reality."[187] He means that the measurements of the fundamental particles of the universe seem to somehow influence the reality that is being observed. On the other hand, Heisenberg argued that "quantum theory does not contain genuine subjective features, it does not introduce the mind of the physicist as a part of the atomic event. But it starts from the division of the world into the 'object' and the rest of the world."[188] Our status as observers results in a particular way in which observations are framed (as objects).

    The uncertainty may lie in our finite abilities to measure and observe. John Polkinghorne explains as follows: "quantum physics should not seek to speak about individual events at all, but its proper concern is with 'ensembles,' that is to say, statistical properties of collections of events."[189] He says that "the wavefunction is not about states of physical systems at all, but about states of the human knowledge of such systems."[190] Does this mean that God knows every quantum detail?

    Some interpret quantum uncertainty as an example of the incredibly interconnected web of reality. Russell calls it the "gossamer-like quality of quantum correlations" and he extrapolates this to "intra-religious unity,"[191] suggesting that our view of God is similarly uncertain because of God's complexity. The complementarity of modern physics resonates particularly well with Daoism. Jiang Sheng says:

> The wholeness of body and soul is the way to be almighty; to be able to grasp the world through keeping the Oneness within (this is just like in quantum physics

---

[186] Ibid., 110-111.
[187] Ibid., 8.
[188] Werner Heisenberg, *Physics and Philosophy* (Prometheus Books, 1999), 55.
[189] Polkinghorne, *Quantum Theory*, 47.
[190] Ibid.
[191] "Quantum physics" in Russell, Stoeger, Coyne, *Physics and Philosophy*, 358.

where the observer and the observed become a whole body).[192]

These metaphorical statements are interesting to contemplate but they are stretching the theoretical concepts quite a bit.

Quantum theory challenges our ordinary view of reality as solid and predictable. Paul Davies describes the Copenhagen interpretation of quantum events in this way: "the concrete matter of daily experience dissolves in a maelstrom of fleeting, ghostly images."[193] It offers a picture of the world in which things are in two places at once, and only probabilities predict where they will eventually end up. Davies also comments that "The quantum factor, however, apparently breaks the chain by allowing effects to occur that have no cause."[194] Polkinghorne suggests that miracles could then be "windows opening up a more profound perspective into the divine reality than that which can be glimpsed in the course of everyday experience."[195] On the other hand, Arthur Peacocke does not see God intervening in quantum events. For God to collapse the wave-function would involve a huge number of interventions for many wave-particles.[196] This kind of intervention also, it should be noted, involves paradoxical time-related problems (which may not be a problem for God, but it disturbs our notion of an orderly universe). Theologically it is difficult to insert God into the indeterminacy at the quantum level. This would require an enormous quantity of interventions if God needs to collapse every wave function. It is an unnecessarily complex way to make things happen, and is compounded by the interactions that must

---

[192] Jiang Sheng, "Daoism and the Uncertainty Principle" in Pranab Das, *Global Perspectives on Science and Spirituality* (Templeton Press, 2009), 84.
[193] Davies, *God and the New Physics,* 102.
[194] Ibid.
[195] John Polkinghorne, *Quantum Physics and Theology,* (Yale University Press, 2007), 36.
[196] Arthur Peacocke, *Paths from Science towards God: The End of all our Exploring* (Oneworld, 2001), 106-7.

ensue in order to carry those changes up to the classical level of molecules and even further to psychological events.

The Copenhagen interpretation puts severe limits on the conclusions that one can draw about the nature of reality itself, since wave-particle duality presents a paradox (which, according to Bohr should shock anyone who understands it!). As well, the standard interpretation takes the wave-function as a probability function. Heisenberg describes it as follows: "The probability function does—unlike the common procedure in Newtonian mechanics—not describe a certain event but, at least during the process of observation, a whole ensemble of possible events."[197] As such, it predicts where a quantum particle will be at any particular time (with the wave equation giving the probabilities for all locations).

What does this do to our view of God? Einstein refused to believe that God would play dice with the universe, putting chance at the bottom level of reality instead of a determinate system. This metaphysical opinion is exactly what is challenged by quantum theory. Perhaps God has created the world with freedom at the bottom level, rather than deterministic equations. How does this change the classical notion of God? Nicholas Saunders notes that most of the theological responses to indeterminacy share the same assumption:

> God's relationship to indeterministic events is such that he has foreknowledge of the consequences of his actions and is capable of interacting with these events. This latter assumption is necessary for God to be able to act purposively and achieve some objective as a result of his action.[198]

In other words, God's omniscience can be maintained in this model (although the future is logically unknowable since it is

---

[197] Heisenberg, 54.
[198] Nicholas Saunders, *Divine Action and Modern Science* (Cambridge University Press, 2002), 125.

indeterminate, and God cannot know something not logically possible).

Quantum mechanics is not as indeterminate as many of its interpreters make it out to be. Saunders notes:

> Looking at the Schrödinger equation from a purely deterministic viewpoint, there is absolutely nothing about this equation (and in consequence the time dependent evolution of any quantum system) that is in any way different from the corresponding situation in classical mechanics).[199]

The mathematical equation gives no fuzzy results: "the wavefunction must be continuous, single-valued, and have a finite value at any particular point."[200] It is like the situation with any probabilistic equations such as those that describe what may happen when a die is cast. The future is indeterminate, and is set out in the probabilities governing the possibility of each event. But we do not create the reality of the die turning up a certain number (maybe you have observed this at the gambling table!).

Heisenberg's famous uncertainty principle fits with a theological view of the transcendence of God. It indicates a lack of human knowledge rather than a lack of determinism in the system that is being described. Saunders notes that Heisenberg used the term 'imprecision' most of the time, rather than indeterminacy.[201] The uncertainty arises as a result of the impossibility of knowing all of the variables (eg. the momentum and position of a particle at the same time). Heinz Pagels explains it this way:

> The randomness at the foundation of the material world does not mean that knowledge is impossible or that physics has failed. To the contrary,... the new quantum theory makes lots of predictions—all in agreement with

---

[199] Ibid., 131.
[200] Ibid., 132.
[201] Ibid., 135.

> experiment. But these predictions are for the distribution of events, not individual events—it is like predicting how many times a specific hand of cards gets dealt on the average. Probability distributions are causally determined, not specific events.[202]

We do not have knowledge of individual events, but there are so many events when we are dealing with collections of atoms in the ordinary world that we can use statistical methods with great accuracy.

The new physics can lead us to see God in a new way. Keith Ward proposes that

> God is the sustainer of a network of dynamic interrelated energies and might well be seen as the ultimate environing non-material field, which draws from material natures a range of the potentialities which are implicit within them.[203]

This sounds rather similar to Arthur Peacocke's notion that God acts in the world as the whole affecting the parts. As well, it is similar to Jurgen Moltmann's idea that God's being 'surrounds' the world but that God contracts so as to create a place within God's being (*tzimtzum*): a field in which this experiment in freedom is taking place.[204]

Similarly, in the Buddhist view: "if the doctrine of *praititya-samatpuda* (dependent co-origination) is correct, then every kind of relation is a cause of suffering and simultaneously an opportunity for enlightenment, which dramatically changes the way we engage the world."[205] Because this religious view does not contain the concept of a god that is in control of

---

[202] Heinz Pagels, "Uncertainty and Complementarity" in Timothy Ferris, *The World Treasury of Physics, Astronomy and Mathematics* (Little, Brown, 1991), 98.
[203] Ward, *God, Chance and Necessity*, 57.
[204] Jurgen Moltmann, *Science and Wisdom* (SCM Press, 2003), 119-120.
[205] Wesley Wildman, "An Introduction to Relational Ontology" in John Polkinghorne, ed. *The Trinity and an Entangled World* (Eerdman's, 2010), 57.

everything there is more emphasis on the nature of the universe itself. The Dalai Lama interprets this as support for the Buddhist idea of interdependence: "we must abolish as a matter of principle the separability of subject and object, and with this all our certainties about the objectifiability of our empirical data."[206] Hindu scriptures also speak of the unity of all things: "'All that is the past, the present and the future, all that is only the syllable *aum.*' ... In other words, cosmic vibrations link both the perceived and unperceived (transcendent) worlds."[207] The spiritual reality that is the basis of existence is seen as the unity of all things (Brahman).

David Bohm argued that "the universe itself is a hologram"[208] (each part contains within itself the whole). He makes a distinction between what he calls the implicate and explicate order (in the first, primary reality is unbroken wholeness, but to our eyes, the explicitly observed world is experienced in separable parts). Diarmid O'Murchu puts it this way:

> Wholeness, which is largely unmanifest and dynamic (not stable) in nature, is the wellspring of all possibility. In seeking to understand life, we begin with the whole, which is always greater than the sum of the parts; paradoxically, the whole is contained in each part, and yet no whole is complete in itself.[209]

This perspective results in a view of the world as subject: creative energy is within the cosmos and there is an evolutionary unfolding of the cosmic dance, a matrix of energy.

---

[206] Dalai Lama, *The Universe in a Single Atom*, (New York: Morgan Road Books, 2005), 52.
[207] Varadaraja V. Raman, "Quantum Mechanics and Some Hindu Perspectives," in *Routledge Companion to Religion and Science*, 165.
[208] Diarmuid O'Murchu, *Quantum Theology* (Crossroad, 1997), 56.
[209] Ibid., 58.

Some interpreters of quantum theory suggest that the indeterminacy of fundamental entities means that multiple universes are possible. In the many-worlds interpretation,

> at every act of measurement, physical reality divides into a multiplicity of separate universes, in each of which different (cloned) experimenters observe the different possible outcomes of the measurement.[210]

On this view, different universes exist encompassing all of the possibilities that are contained in the wafe-function.

If there are multiple universes then it is quite conceivable that life may develop in one of them. But who designed the laws of those universes? Moreover, who designed the laws that make up the possible set of all universes? There must be a God that brings such marvelous things into existence. The atheist could reply: where does that God come from? Must there be a super-God that can bring such a marvelous being into existence? The argument goes on forever. If the chain of causes must stop somewhere, it may as well stop at the universe rather than God.

Theories of physics aim for a Grand Unified Theory. One of these proposals lies in superstring theory, which "assumes that the ultimate building blocks of nature consist of tiny vibrating strings."[211] This mathematical model of the universe uses many dimensions to represent the astounding symmetry that is displayed in the fundamental laws of physics. Unfortunately, string theory is difficult to test experimentally.

Chaos and complexity

When the morning stars together their Creator's glory sang,

---

[210] Polkinghorne, *Quantum Theory*, 52.
[211] Michio Kaku and Jennifer Thompson, *Beyond Einstein* (Anchor Books, 1995), 4.

and the angel host all shouted till with joy the heavens rang,
then your wisdom and your greatness their exultant music told,
all the beauty and the splendor which your mighty works unfold.
Albert F. Bayly

New theories about the interaction of matter are also giving rise to a more complex view of our world and its constituent parts. Chaos theory, for example, provides new explanations for events which had previously been little understood. Rather than giving us a picture of a random universe, chaos theory shows how complex patterns can emerge from the interaction of a few simple elements. Beautiful and unpredictable patterns can result from unexpected sources (for example, the way frost creeps over a window is an unexpected result of the interaction of water condensing onto glass). Scientists can describe the structure of molecules, but they cannot explain life solely in terms of those molecules because they have to account for properties that emerge from the interaction of molecules.

Chaos theory shows that the effects of causes within some systems are wildly unpredictable. This is often called the "butterfly effect," after the image of a butterfly flapping its wings in the Gulf of Mexico and causing a typhoon in India. "An imperceptible change of initial conditions produces a very large effect, the result of the remote butterfly flapping its wings,"[212] writes Alan Cook. Very complex systems like this are dependent on the most infinitesimal changes in their initial conditions. All of these possibilities are embedded within the constitution of the universe itself. We come up against a limit to our knowledge because the equations that describe the complex chain of events are perfectly deterministic. It is, however, impossible for us to

---

[212] Cook, in Watts, 33.

know precisely the initial conditions (after all, we can't watch every butterfly flapping its wings).

Chaos theorists observe patterns arising in the interactions of these complex systems (like the unique shape of every snowflake). Stable forms of behaviour occur; it is not all chaos. These forms arise around what are called "attractors," that is, "a set to which the system evolves after a long enough time."[213] The cosmos is dynamic. It mutates into new forms, but it does so by taking old forms and subjecting them to a kind of testing, by putting them in new contexts. In chaos theory, the environment is a determining influence, since it gives the initial conditions on which the equations act. Similarly, in evolution, the environment changes, and gives new challenges for the multitude of genetic modifications that naturally occur. New environmental niches spawn new organisms that can survive there.

Chaos theory gives us equations which can show us how those interactions are governed (although solving the equations can give different answers if different inputs are given). The systems it examines are not completely anarchic, but instead can be understood according to mathematical equations. However, the equations of complex systems give results that are unexpected, depending on the initial conditions. Natural phenomena that look chaotic, then, are really governed by scientific laws, although they are not deterministic since they are so sensitive to the specific context. Giberson says: "Chaos and quantum uncertainty make it impossible to see the world any longer as determined."[214] Some theologians have used chaos theory to argue for the intervention of God in unexpected ways in our world.

---

[213] https://en.wikipedia.org/wiki/Pullback_attractor
[214] Karl Giberson and Francis Collins, *The Language of Science and Faith* (InterVarsity Press, 2011), 118.

Order can emerge out of seemingly chaotic systems (like the weather). These systems sometimes develop a sort of equilibrium, in which orderly forms emerge out of the maelstrom of events. John Haught, in his summary of viewpoints about science and religion, suggests that it is possible to see matter as "*inherently* self-organizing."[215] This might be seen as a conflict with theology. He goes on: "Hence there is no need for an extraneous, supernatural designer who would put the stamp of order on chaos. Chaos gives rise to order *spontaneously*, and nature blindly selects those systems that are most adaptive."[216] This theory has interesting theological implications:

> Chaos and complexity are stimulating to our theology because they correspond so well with a religious experience that pictures God not only as the source of cosmic order but also as the source of surprise. God in our traditions is, after all, the ultimate origin of the *novelty* that causes chaos or turbulence in the first place.[217]

It looks like God has created a world in which simple natural laws bring about quite complicated things.

Haught sees this as confirmation of the creative activity of God, working through natural laws: "The science of complexity thinks of nature as actively self-creative at all levels."[218] Further, he argues that this makes good theological sense because "it is only because of God's self-emptying love that a self-organizing universe can come into being."[219] God allows things to develop according to their own devices.

"Chaos theory" is more accurately called complexity theory. Philip Clayton explains:

---

[215] John Haught, *Science and Religion: From Conflict to Conversation* (New York: Paulist Press, 1995), 149.
[216] Ibid., 149.
[217] Ibid., 154.
[218] Ibid., 159.
[219] Ibid., 160.

> Phenomena emerge in the development of complex physical systems which, though verifiable through observation, cannot be derived from fundamental physical principles. Even given a complete knowledge of the antecedent states, we would not be able to predict their emergence with the particular qualities they have.[220]

As we understand the laws of nature more adequately, we see a tendency for complicated events and behaviours to be explained in terms of a small set of simple laws. Complexity theory posits a set of equations that generate exceedingly complicated phenomena. Niels Henrik Gregersen argues that

> by focusing on relations and interactions rather than on particular objects, complexity theory supports a shift in world-view from a mechanical clockwork view of the world into an emergentist view of the world as an interconnected network, where flows of information take precedence over localised entities.[221]

This means that nature has within itself the capacity to create higher levels of order.

The Christian view of creation does not mean that God just set the whole thing off, but that God is involved in the universe all the way through (this is known as providence). Arthur Peacocke is a proponent of what he calls "top-down causality." In this model, God is the whole which influences the activity of each of the parts of existence, including our cosmos, which is distinct from God, but within God ("in him we live and move and have our being"). In chaos theory, Peacocke proposes that God sets up the initial conditions so that his desired outcome prevails, without any obvious sign of his intervention (we can

---

[220] Philip Clayton, *Mind and Emergence: From Quantum to Consciousness* (Oxford, 2004), 66.
[221] Niels Henrik Gregersen, "A Primer on Complexity" in Christine Ledger and Stephen Pickard, eds. *Creation and Complexity: Interdisciplinary issues in Science and Religion* (Adelaide: ATF Press, 2004), 14.

never know all of the initial conditions, but God does, and if God changes one butterfly's flying pattern, large changes in the weather can result). Peacocke thinks that we can "regard God as the eternal Creator sustaining in existence processes that are endowed by God with an inherent capability to generate new forms."[222] All of these allow God to act in the universe in miraculous ways, without being obvious about it.

It seems strange for God not to announce his presence, but it seems that God wants us to figure out for ourselves who he is. Chaotic systems are a candidate for the insertion of God's finger into the material and historical process. Modifying the initial conditions in certain select situations could produce massive changes that are foreseen by God's understanding of the equations of complexity. Which situations might pertain? Certainly the weather, but that seems a minor matter, except for the way that it impinges on human history (and it's a clumsy way to change human history). Are there chaotic events in human interactions that also obey complex equations?

This perspective would allow us to see God as part of the system-as-a-whole, influencing the behaviour of individual elements (God knows everything, and how all parts fit into the divine plan—even bad-looking bits). This kind of larger-than-life set of conditions can have a trickle-down effect on particular events in that system. It is an ecological model of the universe as a whole, with God as the source of the entire ecosystem and thus an actor on the highest level.

Instead of the traditional God of order and omniscience, James Huchingson proposes a view of God that includes chaos within God's very being, as the fount of creation's wisdom. He argues, for example, that "God, to be God, must embrace the primordial chaos as integral to God's own being."[223] God selects

---

[222] Peacocke, 92.
[223] James Huchingson, *Pandemonium Tremendum: Chaos and Mystery in the Life of God* (Pilgrim Press, 2001), 117.

among the chaos of possibilities in order to monitor and direct the flow of information through time. In this way "chaos, in its primordial manifestation, is an infinite field of variety, of complete indeterminateness, filled with potency, the source of all created things and one aspect of divine abundance."[224]
Huchingson leaves us with an intriguing picture:

> If God is infinite, and infinity is defined negatively as freedom from all limits and constraints, then chaos, which is just that state, must be present in or to God. Chaos is the infinite reservoir of elemental potentiality. But God is more than this since God is willing, directive and intentional.[225]

It is not clear to me why 'chaos' is used to designate the fecundity of possibilities within God. Why not order? An ordered infinity would work just as well for his theory. A clue is found in the following quotation:

> Divine agency has numerous modes. All have to do with the release of variety into the world in the act of communication. One of the most important modes is to establish a context in which creatures can 'have their being' as well as 'live and move.' God's intention is not to order the world—to design it and then implement that design as *fiat*—but rather, to provide context for the world to design itself in response.[226]

Huchingson's primary commitment lies with the autonomy of creation (especially human beings). Any view of God seen as controlling or limiting our freedom is perceived as demeaning. This God is active, but only in a secondary way: "God is a catalytic agent. God disturbs situations of equilibrium by introducing noise into systems, driving them to higher orders of

---

[224] Ibid., 105.
[225] Ibid., 141.
[226] Ibid., 169.

complexity and stability."[227] There is no personal communication in Huchingson's model, and in this way he does not escape the distant God of deism clothed in process. The liberal hope in progress is assumed in this interplay of freedom amidst an infinity of possibilities. More meditation on the patterns of growth that lead to good configurations would yield a more positive role for God (and perhaps even a realization of the sinful properties of chaos).

Has God let the world run according to this confusion of order and disorder? With a few simple rules applied to a system that includes feedback, the iteration of cycles through time can yield something surprising. But the rules have to be ones that eventually develop some sort of order and the initial parameters have to be tuned correctly. Does this imply a cosmic manager? Gregersen says: "I believe we should see God as continuously creating the world by constituting and supporting self-organising processes."[228] Does God intervene in the microscopic initial conditions so that things turn out right? This seems like an even more deist God than the one who simply lets the world run according to clockwork. At least the rules would yield the appropriate results. God may as well be arbitrary if He is hidden in the void of seemingly random events (in other words, he might as well not exist if He is unobservable).

Freedom seems to be run through with chaos. Emergent order arises out of situations of complexity, in which the laws of nature conspire to interact with the result that new possibilities are born. In short, the future is open because that is the way that our universe is constructed. Perhaps God has made the future unknowable even to its creator. Life is a constant flux, a boiling cauldron of random interactions within a complex network of

---

[227] Ibid., 169.
[228] Niels Hernrik Gregersen, "A World made to Flourish: Divine Design and the Idea of Natural Self-organisation," in Ledger and Pickard, 84.

connections. Order arises spontaneously out of the rules of the interactions between elements.

Does evil emerge from freedom?

Death was not God's doing,
he takes no pleasure in the extinction of the living.
To be—for this he created all;
the world's created things have health in them,
in them no fatal poison can be found,
and Hades holds no power on earth.
Wisdom 1:13-14

If natural laws enable the formation of more complicated structures within nature (that is, physical arrangements of physical components), what room is there for God? All of the causes we see must have some cause. If we accept that God created a universe that can self-organize and create through its own natural processes, then what are we to make of those complicated structures and processes? There are wondrous examples of complexity such as the eye, the cell, DNA and the mind. If the world unfolds through its own processes, then what about earthquakes, hurricanes, disease and torture? Do these come from the mind of God as well?

The usual Christian answer is to say that the maladjustments of the system are only a perversion of the good creation (using the goodness of reality in bad ways). If God created free beings, then they can choose evil as well as good. According to the emergentist view, does this evil lie within themselves in some way, only to be actuated by some context or accident of history? Isn't God ultimately responsible for embedding this possibility in the universe?

We can thus see all of nature as the work of God. Philip Clayton puts it this way: "the amazing fecundity of natural evolution in the end expresses the intentional creative structuring of God."[229] Eastern Orthodox theologians seem more comfortable with this notion than Western Christians. They make a distinction between the unknowable God and his actions in the universe. Kallistos Ware says:

> In his essence God is infinitely transcendent, utterly beyond all created being, beyond all understanding and all participation from the human side. But in his energies—which are nothing else than God himself in action—God is inexhaustibly immanent, maintaining all things in being, animating them, making each of them a sacrament of his dynamic presence.[230]

It is not that God forces nature to do his will but that nature itself displays the being of God (fully but not essentially).

Ware acknowledges the problem of evil and gives the traditional Christian response: "Evil is no more than a parasite, a twisting and distortion of things that, in their essential nature as created by God, are fundamentally good."[231] Of course, God could have constructed a universe without the possibility of radical freedom (I mean freedom also for particles and molecules to move and bond in unexpected, unpredictable, even indeterminate ways). Such a universe, Christian theology claims, would not have free creatures able to love God (or reject him).

Another possibility lies in the traditional Chinese concept of yin-yang. This idea permeates Eastern religions in various forms but essentially it emphasizes the intertwining of opposites. You cannot have good without evil and in a strange way they are interacting or even complementary forces. ☯

---

[229] Philip Clayton, "Emergence from Quantum Physics to Religion: A Critical Appraisal," in Clayton and Davies, 319.
[230] Kallistos Ware, "God Immanent yet Transcendent: The Divine Energies according to Saint Gregory Palamas" in Clayton and Peacocke, 160.
[231] Ware, 167.

Psychology and sociology: psyche and spirit

O the mind, mind has mountains; cliffs of fall
Frightful, sheer, no-man-fathomed. Hold them cheap
May who ne'er hung there. Nor does long our small
Durance deal with that steep or deep.
Gerard Manley Hopkins, "No worst, there is none"

The mind is a mystery, a wonder to behold. For much of Christian history, the mind was seen as the soul since reason was considered to be the image of God. How is scientific study of the brain affecting our view of the rational seat of human nature? Psychologists see the brain as a network of neurons, a biological machine for processing information. The bodily basis for mind is stressed, as scientists search for the natural mechanisms of thought. Fraser Watts argues that the concept of 'self' has largely replaced the old theological 'soul.'[232] However, spirit is again being considered as a dimension of human experience,

---

[232] Fraser Watts, *Theology and Psychology* (Ashgate, 2002), 63. Watts actually views this as a helpful development, but others argue that modern psychology is overly obsessed with the self: see Paul Vitz, *Psychology as Religion: The Cult of Self-worship* (W.B. Eerdmans, 1994) or Mark R. McMinn, *Care for the Soul: Exploring the Intersection of Psychology & Theology* (InterVarsity Press, 2001).

intertwined with body and mind. In medical fields, the interconnection of mind and body is being explored.

The history of psychology is a fascinating study since it is intertwined with religion and philosophy. Psychology has often had a mythic element and is sometimes expressed in literary modes. Karl Jaspers argued that human consciousness experienced a "great leap forward" in which "man becomes conscious of Being as a whole."[233] He called this the axial period and identified it around 800-200 BC because history shows an awakening to a spiritual consciousness in various places around the world independently (Confucius, Lao Tzu, Buddha, Hebrew prophets, Greek philosophers like Aristotle).[234]

The mythic roots of our study of the mind remained a fruitful source for those who wished to analyze human behaviour. Astrology can be seen as a religious psychology. While Christian thinkers repudiated the astrological signs, their understanding of mental processes was often expressed in equally religious terms. The medieval mind, for example, was seen as affected by demons, which could be interpreted as a religious explanation of human behaviours, especially madness. Ill health was often seen as a result of sin. Salvation was sometimes seen as "the cure of the soul" which was beset by these mysterious forces: physical and spiritual.

There are various ways to interpret this, and indeed the various religions developed their own ways of thinking about this larger spiritual reality (also seen as internal to us). One option is is typified by Hindu non-dualism (Advaita): to see the internal reality of the self as intrinsically connected to the larger spiritual reality. In the Hindu tradition, this strand insists that "there is a reality, other than this, which is the causal basis of our separate individuality. This life is not self-existent."[235] This

---

[233] Harold Schilling, *New Consciousness in Science and Religion*, 19.
[234] Ibid.
[235] Keith Ward, *Religion and Human Nature* (Clarendon Press, 1988), 11.

interpretation is most clearly seen in the Upanishads, where the central insight is 'that thou art' (you are essentially identical with Brahman, the spiritual source of everything). In a modern revival of this tradition, Vivekenanda says: "[Y]ou are all gods."[236] It would be more accurate to say that within each person there is a spark of divinity because it is quite obvious that we do not have superpowers. The Advaita tradition poses some problems theologically as well because it raises the question about where evil comes from. It would seem necessary to conclude that "God (Brahman) is free from illusion and evil."[237] Are we also, then?

There are within the Hindu tradition completely opposite interpretations (dualist). This option is most clearly seen in the avatars of Vishnu. One of them, Krishna is seen as the "true ultimate agent of creaturely actions."[238] According to this view, there are "an infinite number of centres of consciousness, eternally distinct, which are not omnipotent or omniscient, and whose function is to serve the supreme Lord in loving devotion."[239] Even more broadly seen, "[T]he Lord is the material cause of every universe."[240] In other words, the reality of the gods (especially Brahman, the spirit that is manifested in all of the Hindu personifications of gods) is metaphysically distinct from our reality.

According to the monist view, the spiritual essence of the universe (Brahman) is expressed in many ways in the reality in which we find ourselves. It is a beautiful concept: "the world can also be seen as the divine play, in which the One, though remaining complete in itself, manifests in diversity so as to realize its infinite potential in endless ways."[241] This idea has also been expressed in the Western tradition by Hegel: "the

---

[236] Ibid., 12.
[237] Ibid., 14.
[238] Ibid., 38.
[239] Ibid., 41.
[240] Ibid., 37.
[241] Ibid., 15.

whole historical process of the realm of appearances was possibly an appearing in terms of what the Absolute Reality in itself really is."[242] From the Advaita Hindu perspective, there is an "irreconcilable identity-in-difference"[243] in all things. This view makes little sense from the Western view of the individuality of selves but the Eastern idea of reincarnation puts a different spin on it. Throughout many lifetimes, "souls can learn to love"[244] even though there is "forgetfulness of one's past lives."[245] This view also means that human beings should feel no desire because they are part of a universal spiritual existence requiring no sensual pleasure.

  Buddhists have a view of the self that is quite different than the typically Western dualistic split between body and soul. The spiritual aspect of the person is inseparable from the body (although it can be instantiated in different bodies, this actually shows how the body is integrally connected to the spiritual side of our being. Buddhism emphasizes liberation from self through an active program in this life. Buddhist philosophy developed a rather advanced metaphysical framework in order to make sense of this state of things. Not just individuals, but "all compounded things are impermanent, all states are devoid of self."[246] In us, this means that "the collection of aggregates which constitutes the empirical self gives rise to a karmic continuation in another physical form."[247] Reincarnation poses a bit of problem conceptually in this way of thinking because there is no continuous identity (Buddhists call it *anatman* (no-self) to distinguish it from the Hindu concept of atman, the deepest self that is sustained through different lives). One way to explain this in Buddhism is to see ourselves as a "continuation of a series of

---

[242] Ibid., 25.
[243] Ibid., 37.
[244] Ibid., 62.
[245] Ibid., 64.
[246] Ibid., 79.
[247] Ibid., 80.

continuous, transient, and causally connected states."[248]
Buddhists call this the "subtle body," that is, mental dispositions to act that produce merit (karma).

Philosophy and psychology

What is matter? Never mind.
What is mind? No matter.
Anonymous

The study of the mind was at first principally carried out by philosophers. The primary method was introspection (observing themselves think). Many theologians participated in this study, notably Augustine, whose *Confessions* includes a classic study of memory. Historically, philosophical accounts of the mind's workings have been an integral part of the way in which we view the world.

The example of Descartes is instructive. In his central insight ("I think, therefore I am"),[249] his introspection led him to conclude that he could not doubt his own existence (rather than starting with his physical existence and concluding that he therefore is able to think, a more common-sense approach). This formulation of the relation of our minds to the world formed centuries of philosophical thought. As well, Descartes's insight founded the next couple of centuries of study of the mind, for he concluded that our mind was distinct from our brain (thus separating the spiritual from the merely mental).

The study of psychology is closely and naturally linked to philosophy, as is apparent in the thought of Sigmund Freud. His theories of the mind were developed from observation of a rather narrow spectrum of patients, and yet he drew the most

---

[248] Ibid.
[249] Rene Descartes, "Discourse on Method" (available at http://www.gutenberg.org/ebooks/59)

general conclusions about human nature from this sample (a rather unscientific procedure). He also applied his theory to religion in a reductionist way in his classic *The Future of an Illusion*, explaining religious experiences as manifestations of unconscious desires or needs. His student, Carl Jung, was more sympathetic to religion, analyzing the mythical roots of observations of human behaviour. He argued that ancient myths contain great truths about the human spirit. He sought to uncover archetypes of the 'collective unconscious,' positing that all human beings have common experiences underneath our cultural differences.

These psychological theories were more philosophical than scientific in nature not only in their method but also in their far-reaching and universal conclusions about human nature. Psychologists slowly came to adopt the central tenets of the scientific method: repeatable experiments, careful observation and rigorous testing of hypotheses. In addition, the biological foundations of the mind began to be explored in much more detail using the advanced instruments provided by medical technology.

These developments have exacerbated the division between the mind and the brain. Many scientists simply study the brain, seeing no need to assume an invisible spirit inside the head, directing mental processes. In a way, psychology simply identifies the mind with the brain, explaining all mental processes as biological interactions. Francis Crick, one of the discoverers of DNA, presents this astonishing hypothesis:

> You, your joys and your sorrows, your memories and your ambitions, your sense of personal identity and free will, are in fact no more than the behavior of a vast assembly of nerve cell and their associated molecules.[250]

---

[250] Francis Crick, *The Astonishing Hypothesis: The Scientific Search for the Soul* (Scribner, 1994), 3.

Crick's view fails to give credit to the wonderful kinds of behaviours of which we are capable. Roger Penrose, in contrast, has argued that the brain contains quantum events (at the level of microtubules).[251] This would introduce indeterminacy into our thought processes (at least at the unconscious level). It is, however, difficult to see how we could study quantum behaviour within the brain.

Contemporary neurological studies show more promise in revealing how the brain works. Steven Pinker argues that "the mind is what the brain does."[252] He argues that thinking is a form of computation but, in a curious reversal, the computer is not a model for thinking. Instead, Marvin Minsky's society of mind pictures the modules of the mind working on sub-problems.[253] The brain is wired differently than a computer because of the massive interconnectivity of the neurons. However, it is not the number of neurons but their arrangement that makes the brain so powerful. For example, the logic 'gates' built in neural networks are multi-level arrangements strengthened by association and repetition.[254]

Pinker engages in 'reverse-engineering' the cognitive structures in which we engage. In this way, he participates in the cognitive revolution, which moves beyond the behaviourism that saw the human mind as a black box, and only analyzed it in terms of inputs and outputs (stimuli and responses). In a way, however, neurological analyses of the brain simply put the stimulus-response model down a level (the black boxes are inside the brain, which cognitive processes use as sub-modules like the algorithm libraries available to computer programmers in high-level programming languages. For example, short-term

---

[251] Roger Penrose, *Shadows of the Mind: A Search for the Missing Science of Consciousness*. Oxford University Press, 1994
[252] Steven Pinker, *How the Mind Works* (W. W. Norton, 1997), 21.
[253] Marvin Minsky, *The Society of Mind* (Simon & Schuster, 1986).
[254] Pinker, 100.

memory becomes a process that relies on the visual and phonological encoding done in various locations of the brain.

Current artificial intelligence researchers are trying to build massively interconnected parallel processing 'neural networks.' The brain has had millions of years of evolution to grow the most optimal processes for doing such elemental tasks as face recognition (which we do almost instantaneously). Pinker's book is devoted to this sort of evolutionary psychology and he emphasizes the specific capacities that the human brain has evolved. He argues that a circular feedback process developed in which activities like seeing, walking, hunting, and relating in groups developed certain areas of the brain and thus enabled particular cognitive patterns. For example, mental images (and their rotation) are made possible by the structure of our eyes as well as the way that we can manipulate objects with our hands.[255]

Pinker thinks that the mind still needs higher-order cognitive representations (and the patterns of relationships between them). In order to understand a language one must not only process the symbols adequately so as to produce sentences but also do some sort of internal non-computational process that allows for creative interpretation and construction of new ideas. He says: "Visual thinking is often driven more strongly by the conceptual knowledge we use to organize our images than by the contents of the images themselves."[256] This requires a linguistic structure that allows us to interpret the "blooming, buzzing confusion" (William James' phrase) of our sensory stimuli.

These developments need not deter us from thinking about the relation between our spirit and our brain. The question about our human identity remains a religious question even if we see the mind as purely biological. We should think about the

---

[255] Pinker, 279-284.
[256] Ibid., 295.

spiritual dimension of our lives as it is manifested in our bodies and experiences.

Neurotheology (minds, brains and religious experiences)

The highest activities of consciousness have their origins in physical occurrences of the brain just as the loveliest melodies are not too sublime to be expressed by notes.
Somerset Maugham

The brain is a marvelously complicated structure. It is massively interconnected because every neuron can have a link to many others (each neuron is like a website with links to many other sites). Some suggest that the number of connections in a single brain outnumbers the number of atoms in the entire universe. But it is not the sheer number of connections that makes a difference; it is the way that they are organized. Good connections are reinforced and bad ones wither away. The brain has a plasticity that allows it to adapt to its environment. The structures of memory and language acquisition, visual processing and cognitive evaluation guide this development as the brain learns more and more how to function well.

Stephen Pinker's proposal of several mental modules combines the complicated interconnections of neurons into functioning patterns of activity. For example, one relatively basic cognitive process involves visual perception (the organization of the "blooming, buzzing confusion" of colour patches). Pinker argues that the brain is hard-wired to parse the mass of information coming through its eyes. For example, babies learn 'object permanence' (the principle that an object still exists although hidden) very early on. It is hard-wired into our genetic structure that brains develop this module in order to deal with a world in which objects sometimes disappear from view. Memory is vital to this process, and yet it seems to be a distinct process in the brain, interacting with the visual input from the optic nerve, as well as cognitive pattern-matching modules (which Pinker describes at length). [257] Pinker argues that the structure of our brain indicates a sort of trial-and-error process such as evolution, although there are many gaps in any possible explanation, given our lack of knowledge of earlier brain structures (which were, after all, not preserved).

Examination of religious impulses has recently delved into the lowest levels of brain processing. Philip Clayton outlines some possible intersections between neuroscience and theology. He proposes a middle path between reductionism and dualism, which he calls "emergentist supervenience."[258] This solution to the interminable mind-brain problem sees the mind as a function of the brain, but a function which 'supervenes' on its lower operations. In other words, the mind has its own level of functioning which is not solely dependent on the biochemical events happening in the skull.

This two-level approach does not posit a dualism between mind and matter (two ontologically different substances). But it is more than a two-aspect theory, in which the physical events in the brain are simply interpreted as mental actions when looked at from a different perspective. Mental events have some independent status because they influence the patterns of interactions at the neural level. A memory, for example, is not just the residue of impulses mapping out a pathway through a set of neurons, but a vivid impression of a past event.

This way of looking at the brain-mind connection is theologically necessary, argues Fraser Watts, because it lies

---

[257] Pinker, 211-299.
[258] Philip Clayton, "Neuroscience, the Person and God: An Emergentist Account" in Robert Russell, Nancey Murphy, Theo Meyering, Michael Arbib, eds. *Neuroscience and the Person: Scientific Perspectives on Divine Action* (Vatican Observatory, 1999), 199.

between the two mistakes of seeing our relation to God as purely spiritual and the position that God 'tweaks' our thoughts by meddling in the neural pathways (God of the synapses). This view is also important because it widens our perspective on what constitutes a human person. The 'image of God' has often been seen as our rationality, which leaves some human beings without that image (those in a coma, infants, etc.). Watts suggests that "God could presumably act in relation to people who, through incapacity, had no conscious awareness of anything."[259] This would require some sort of direct brain stimulation, perceived unconsciously.

Some researchers have attempted to locate precisely the part of the brain that is involved in religious experience. Ramachandran claims to have located the "God-spot: he reports that "patients with lesions in the lower temporal region of their brain tended to have intense religious experiences."[260] Michael Persinger artificially induced religious experiences with a helmet feeding impulses to the temporal lobe.[261] Oliver Sacks interpreted Hildegard of Bingen's visions as migraine headaches.[262] More recent research proposes that there is no single "God-spot." Instead, parts of the brain work together in the process of interpreting religious experience.[263]

Fraser Watts argues that "[T]here is a particular kind of consciousness involved in spirituality. It is through our consciousness that we come to have an awareness of God, or

---

[259] Fraser Watts, "Cognitive Neuroscience and Religious Consciousness" in Russell et al, 327.
[260] Philip Clayton, *Religion and Science: The Basics* (Routledge, 2013), 114.
[261] Jack Hitt, "This is your Brain on God" *Wired* 7.11 Nov. 1999. http://www.wired.com/wired/archive/7.11/persinger.html
[262] Oliver Sacks, "The Visions of Hildegard" in *The Man who Mistook his Wife for a Hat* (London: Duckworth, 1985).
[263] Nigel Barbour, "The God-spot Revisited" https://www.psychologytoday.com/blog/the-human-beast/201208/the-god-spot-revisited

divinity."[264] He suggests that we think scientifically about brain processes, but interpret them theologically: "The neurological theory becomes an account of the natural processes by which the real God makes himself known."[265] The brain is thus seen as a vessel for God's communication to humans.

Buddhist theories of the mind have traditionally been attentive to the role of the spirit in the human person (although not linking that to a personal conception of God). As a result, techniques of meditation have been developed in order to aid humans in their personal (spiritual) development. The current Dalai Lama promotes neurological investigation as a corollary to these spiritual techniques. He thinks that both religion and science can enhance "the cultivation of a compassionate heart and the cultivation of deep insights into the nature of reality."[266] Buddhists use "mindfulness" to achieve greater spiritual understanding.

Eugene D'Aquili and Andrew Newberg, using their research on Catholic nuns and Buddhist monks, propose a unified theory of religious experience that avoids the localisation of other researchers. They suggest two conceptual operations that involve a range of brain functions: first, the causal operator (seeing the world as controlled by God), and second, the holistic operator (a sense of unity especially in mystical experience).[267] Their proposal attempts to explain wildly diverse religious experiences through a single psychological mechanism.

Neurological attempts to analyze religious experience might explain it away or they might simply point to the brain activity that is happening when mystical experience occurs.

---

[264] Fraser Watts, "Brain, Mind and Soul" in Fraser Watts, ed. *Science Meets Faith* (SPCK, 1998), 61.
[265] Ibid., 70.
[266] Tenzin Gyatso, the Dalai Lama, "Science at the Crossroads," http://www.dalailama.com/messages/buddhism/science-at-the-crossroads
[267] Eugene D'Aquili and Andrew Newberg, *Why God Won't Go Away: Brain Science and the Biology of Belief* (Ballantine Books, 2001).

D'Aquili and Newberg cautiously explore the latter possibility, saying that

> genuine mystical encounters ... are not necessarily the result of emotional distress or neurotic delusion or any pathological state at all. Instead, they may be produced by sound, healthy minds coherently reacting to perceptions that in neurobiological terms are absolutely real.[268]

Their research on Catholic nuns and Buddhist monks indicates a common neurological activity, which they describe as an erasure of the boundaries of the self and a consequent feeling of being united with everything that is. John Hick takes this a step further and argues that religious experiences from around the world point to the same conclusion: human minds are in touch with a Reality more fundamental than our ordinary one.[269] However, he argues that "[T]he unity experienced by the [Christian] mystics is not a unity of being but a union of wills in which the human is fully conformed to the divine."[270] It would be necessary to examine various religious interpretations of mystical experience in order to fully catalogue the ways in which activities of the mind are interpreted religiously.

Psychology and theology

God of the earth, the sky, the sea!
Maker of all, above below!
creation lives and moves in thee,
they present life through all doth flow.
We give thee thanks, thy name we sing!
Almighty God, our praise we bring.

---

[268] D'Aquili and Newberg, 100.
[269] John Hick, *The New Frontier of Religion and Science: Religious Experience, Neuroscience and the Transcendent* (Palgrave Macmillan, 2006).
[270] Hick, 23.

But higher far and far more clear,
thee in our spirit we behold;
thine image and thyself are there,
th'indwelling God, proclaimed of old.
Samuel Longfellow

Moving upwards to higher levels of cognitive functioning, some psychologists examine the role of religious ideas in the way people think consciously. David Myers and Malcolm Jeeves ask the question: "Should there be a Christian psychology?"[271] For example, should we analyze the human being as a self or a soul? These are not mutually exclusive options, they think, but different dimensions that need exploration with distinct procedures. Just as the other sciences can be seen as levels of explanation (of atoms, molecules, organisms, living beings), psychology should be seen as a limited explanation of human existence. We need theology to complete this picture, since it includes the widest context, namely God.

There are many suspicions about religion from a psychological perspective.[272] For example, guilt can become a neurotic condition if it is excessive, although in the right 'dose' it is useful if it tells us that we're doing something wrong. The modern preoccupation with self-esteem may be a healthy perspective or it may develop into an overweening pride in our own capacity to act and control our life. The characteristics of a good counselor, such as warmth, empathy, and genuineness are like Christian love in their concern for the other (similar to C. S. Lewis's analysis of the concept of *agape*),[273] but they may descend into a lack of judgment or moral evaluation of a person's action.

---

[271] David Myers and Malcolm Jeeves, *Psychology Through the Eyes of Faith* (Christian College Coalition, 1987).
[272] Fraser Watts, *Theology and Psychology*, 5.
[273] C. S. Lewis, *The Four Loves* (Harcourt, Brace, 1960). See also Anders Nygren, *Agape and Eros* (SPCK, 1982).

We could compare the evolutionary model of psychology to the Christian conception of sin. Watts remarks that "the evolution of moral consciousness makes it possible to do wrong with a new kind of deliberateness."[274] He has some criticisms of evolutionary Christologies if they see Christ as the culmination of creation instead of rescuing us from the fall. In particular, Teilhard de Chardin's view of the inevitability of spiritualization of the cosmos seems too optimistic, and does not really give a role to Christ (especially in the sense of Barth's transcendent God breaking into human existence and altering our ontological condition—making us a new creation).

Has psychology reduced our talk about the soul to the activities of the brain? Jeeves proposes that we now work the other way: first we must understand the brain, and how it is intricately linked to the mind, and then we can talk about how we are constituted as souls.[275] He shows how bottom-up processes build the mental experience of an individual, while the mental experiences modify the events going on in the brain.

The structure of the neuronal connections is constantly modified by the conscious attention we give to particular experiences. Robert Pollack points out that

> There are about three billion letters in the human genome. But there about a million-fold more synaptic connections in a human brain at birth than there are letters in any human cell's canonical text. These synaptic connections—the basis of all mental activity later in life—cannot have all been specifically encoded by our genomes. ...
>
> Our DNA encodes, in other words, a Learning Machine. ... The mature brain forever retains plasticity in its circuits, and it never loses the capacity to link past

---

[274] Watts, 116.
[275] Malcolm Jeeves, "Mind Reading and Soul Searching in the Twenty-first Century" in Joel Green, ed. *What About the Soul?* (Nashville: Abingdon Press, 2004).

> with present experience by familiarity of synaptic pattern. Synaptic connections are made and broken throughout life."[276]

In other words, our brain is constantly being rewired by our experiences and how we interpret them.

Is there any personal agency if our minds are controlled by these subconscious agents? Jeeves argues that the very complexity of the brain mitigates against such a conclusion. Our personal agency is a peculiar combination of brain events, including conscious decisions and judgments about how we interpret our world and ourselves. There may be no place in the brain that holds the "I" (a CEO ghost in the machine), but instead Jeeves sees the "I" as the self that is constituted by the combination of events that go on inside the head.

We are not just biological machines nor are we determined by our neural networks. Jeeves gives the example of "mirror neurons"[277] as a particularly helpful brain structure that constitutes a very human experience: empathy. Our brains fire the same pathways that are engaged in a person that we are observing. In other words, we are hard-wired to be able to imagine ourselves in another person's experience. The Christian view of the person is grounded in God's personal being (the inter-relationship of the Trinity). From an Eastern Orthodox perspective, John Zizioulas argues that "only theology can treat of the genuine, the authentic person, because the authentic person, as absolute ontological freedom, must be 'uncreated,' that is, unbounded by any 'necessity,' including its own existence."[278] Gareth Jones argues that we are an astounding creation made by God to be free within a complex

---

[276] Robert Pollack, "A Place for Religion in Science?" *CrossCurrents* 55:2 (Summer 2005), 262.
[277] Jeeves, 24.
[278] John Zizioulas, *Being as Communion* (St. Vladimir's Seminary Press, 1985), 43.

interconnection of material structures.[279] Only this process can produce conscious beings able to relate to the God who created them. All of this brain-talk is not reductionist since it suggests that our self is the product of the interaction of mind and body with the world and other beings.

Development and personality

Man may be defined as the animal that can say "I," that can be aware of himself as a separate entity.
Erich Fromm

The basic theological questions are: Who am I? Where did I come from? Where am I going? Paul Gauguin has a painting with a similar title: "Where do we come from? What are we? Where are we going?"[280] It illustrates the fundamental questioning that each human person goes through. Harold Faw surveys a number of psychological theories that can be used in understanding ourselves and relates them to Christian themes. He mentions the theory of Abraham Maslow, in which there is a hierarchy of needs. First, basic physiological necessities must be present in order for human beings to merely survive (food, water, sex!). If these are satisfied, then social needs can be addressed, such as intimacy and family. The highest need for Maslow is the desire for self-actualization.[281] This includes career aspirations and identity construction. Where is God in this picture of the human being? Is self-actualization the highest human achievement?

Developmental theories chart the growth that human beings undergo. For example, Piaget identified cognitive stages in the infant: sensorimotor, pre-operational, concrete operational,

---

[279] Gareth Jones, "A Neurobiological Portrait of the Human Person" in Green, 39.
[280] "Paul Gauguin," *Wikipedia*. http://en.wikipedia.org/wiki/Paul_Gauguin
[281] Harold Faw, *Psychology in Christian perspective* (Baker Books, 1995), 101.

formal operational. Erik Erikson's model presents fundamental conflicts that must be resolved in order for the human being to progress towards a health and fulfilled life. For example, in adolescence, identity is formed as the individual learns to progress from the roles largely defined by their parents towards a self-chosen model of his or her own self-image. For example, he delineates a series of conflicts to be resolved (eg. trust vs mistrust) as the person moves through the life-cycle.[282]

Does this analysis of life stages completely explain the human struggle to become a whole person? Where is the soul in this? Is there a spiritual dimension to the human being that also needs to be a stage of development? Faw notes a distinction between two views of personhood: functional and intrinsic.[283] The first sees the person as a function of biochemical interactions in the brain, while the second sees the person as the essential category through which we must consider human life. There is a mystery about human beings that cannot be fully explained by science. "We are fearfully and wonderfully made" (Psalm 139:14).

Faw notes the usefulness of trait theory, which can identify characteristic behaviours of the person. There are deep-seated and largely unconscious patterns of response that we use, some given by our genetic make-up and others developed by the nurture of our parents or the habitual patterns ingrained in our society. Current psychological theories of personality use a combination of five tendencies to characterize different patterns of behaviour.[284]

The Myers-Briggs personality temperament categorization tries to identify four personality traits that people

---

[282] See "Erikson's Development Stages" from "Patient Teaching," Loose Leaf Library Springhouse Corporation (1990).
http://honolulu.hawaii.edu/intranet/committees/FacDevCom/guidebk/teachtip/erikson.htm
[283] Faw, 58.
[284] See "Five-factor Model." http://www.personalityresearch.org/bigfive.html

display in their basic reactions to the world around them and to other people. These can be used to identify how we function (sub-consciously) and to a certain extent act the way that we do. Keirsey and Bates identify each type with a particular saint who represents a specific theological approach.[285] Do different people relate to God in different ways? What does this mean for the church? We should study these 'types' so that we can understand why other people view God in different ways. All of us have to be aware that we often project our own understanding of ourselves onto God (seeing God in our image). This can cause conflict and theological disagreements that are based on our own inadequate understanding of the diversity of human nature.

Carl Jung's theory identified the complementarity of opposites. We should strive to recognize that we have negative traits in ourselves that we vilify (unconsciously projecting them onto others). Jung encourages us to embrace the shadow side of our personality (as well as the animus/anima complementarity) in order to fully integrate the different aspects of ourselves, and not project our fears about our dark side onto other people (thus creating suspicion and mistrust, even violence).

William James, in his seminal book, *The Varieties of Religious Experience*, was very aware of the various ways in which religious experience manifests itself. His interviews with religious people give a more adequate sense of the subjective experience that happens in these cases. He notes a major category of religious experience which he calls the religion of healthy-mindedness: "grateful admiration of the gift of so happy an existence."[286] These "once-born," as he calls them, "see God, not as a strict Judge, ... but as the animating spirit of a beautiful

---

[285] Jon Noring, "A Summary of Personality Typing." http://www.ibiblio.org/pub/academic/psychology/alt.psychology.personality/FAQ.almost
[286] William James, *The Varieties of Religious Experience* (Random House, 1902), 77.

harmonious world."[287] Another type of individual has a more complicated cognitive relationship to God because he speculates that they have a divided self: "wayward impulses disrupt their most deliberate plans."[288] For some, religion is a "one-step forward, two-steps back" kind of experience.

James saw conversion as a growth-crisis. It imitates the development in adolescents of a change in identity from child to adult. He argues that

> what is attained is often an altogether new level of spiritual vitality, a relative heroic level, in which impossible things have become possible and new energies and endurances are shown. The personality is changed, the man *is* born anew.[289]

James identifies two types of conversion. One is the sudden, spontaneous, instantaneous reversal of life. The other is a slower process, more voluntary, in which habitual actions more gradually bring about the religious mindset.

Theology and therapy

'Tis education forms the common mind,
Just as the twig is bent, the tree's inclined.
Alexander Brown

Fundamental assumptions guide the thought of religion and psychology. Don Browning argues that humanistic psychologies are based on the idea that harmony can be achieved through self-actualization.[290] Integration of the disparate impulses within us is necessary in order to become a healthy and well-balanced person. Dysfunctions like anxiety are socially induced by the

---

[287] Ibid., 79.
[288] Ibid., 166.
[289] Ibid., 236.
[290] Don Browning and Terry Cooper, *Religious Thought and the Modern Psychologies* (Fortress Press, 2004), 61.

imposition of parents, authority figures and peers. There is tremendous optimism embedded in this view: the belief in the natural state of the human being.

In contrast, Reinhold Niebuhr argues that "man is insecure and involved in natural contingency."[291] Christians see human existence as tragically coloured by sin. Human beings are selfish and strive to secure their own existence, beset on all sides as we are by the forces of nature and society. The moral development theory of Kohlberg is noted by Faw as a helpful way to think about how human beings come to be the kind of creatures that we can be. His perspective shows that human beings are motivated by several different factors in their actions towards others. At the most basic level, the consequences of our actions are mirrored back to us by others ("an eye for an eye"). Thomas Hobbes called it a "war of all against all" in his monumental book, *Leviathan*. The social contract of Johnn Locke represents an ascent to a higher level since the state takes into its hand the role of punishment. This allows each individual to 'give up' the right of retribution into an impersonal authority, which preserves the 'justice' of punishment, but removes it from the vigilante structure of personal revenge. In this level, we come to respect the law as an entity in itself.

The highest level of moral reasoning, according to Kohlberg, is one in which actions are guided by principle. He gives the example of the Golden Rule: "Do unto others as you would have them do unto you." This command has often been compared to Kant's principle of universalizability. In Kant's view, every moral action could be expressed as the result of a maxim (or rule), and good actions were those whose maxims could be adopted by anyone.

Does this explanation of human morality correspond to the Christian one? It is intriguing that Jesus' commandment to "do unto others as you would have them do unto you" is

---

[291] Ibid., 77.

included in Kohlberg's highest level of moral development. It is a good ethical guideline that anyone, even non-Christians, can follow, because it requires us to imagine how our own moral rule would work if it were applied to us by another person.

Another Christian analysis of human existence, that of Soren Kierkegaard, emphasizes the anxiety that we feel—a dread directed not at any particular fear-generating object, but a generalized sense of our own finiteness in the infinite cosmos. In relation to God, we are even more anxious, since God's ways are beyond ours (especially the ethical ones, as illustrated by the 'knights of faith' in *Fear and Trembling*). All we can do as human beings is summed up in the figure of the knights of infinite resignation: resigned to our place in the cosmos 'betwixt and between' matter and spirit.

Browning goes on to discuss therapies that aim to heal the human psyche. All of the theories discussed above provide models of how human beings should develop, and so can be applied in counseling situations in order to direct patients towards the goal of health and well-being. It is often difficult, however, to get people to change. We are comfortable in our settled habits of action, even if they are not helpful or even self-destructive.

Victor Turner suggests that in order for change to happen, we must separate ourselves from our past self-conception and move into a liminal stage. This boundary situation (perhaps a breakdown or a crisis) forces us to re-evaluate ourselves and confront startling revelations or uncomfortable realizations. In so doing, however, we can develop a new framework in which we collect some positive habits of thought (especially positive self-talk). Browning affirms that "for many individuals experiencing mild self-confusion or fragmentation over value conflicts these therapies may be particularly powerful in providing the psychological space necessary for the arousal of deeper capacities for freedom, initiative and agency."[292] However, he is critical of Turner's lack of recognition of the need to also re-affirm old values that were important to the former self. We can never (and should not) completely break from the past, but we need to integrate those positive gifts that have been given to us. Carl Rogers applied this view of the importance of the self to therapy, insisting on the necessity of giving unconditional regard to the patient. His client-centred therapy refused to impose the views of the counselor or psychologist on the patient, instead guiding him or her to develop their own solutions to their problems.

In all of these views of the human being, the modern metaphor of the self seems to dominate. In the Christian view, however, we come to our complete fulfillment in our relation to God. Browning notes that we need to consider God in many dimensions: creator, judge, redeemer. There is a human analogue to each of these aspects of God's character: grace, sin, healing. Browning mentions the Jewish theologian Martin Buber, who proposed that the human-God relation is best described as an 'I-Thou' situation (using the intimate second-person singular found in many European languages). It is this personal relationship to God that grounds Christian thinking about psychology.

There are several human activities that flow from our concept of God and our relationship with him. For example, *agape* is the self-sacrificial attitude that takes no thought of self when caring for the other.[293] Anders Nygren, in his classic study of Christian love, describes it as "spontaneous, free, disinterested and totally unpredicated upon the value of the object of love."[294] This is the other side of the command to "love your neighbour as yourself." The other person has value because they are also created in the image of God as a centre of personality and intention. This leads us to equal regard of all persons. When

---

[292] Browning, 83.
[293] Ibid., 131.
[294] Ibid., 134.

Christians think about virtue, they do not necessarily see it as effective. In other words, we do the right thing because it is good not because it will help us. God commands us to love our enemies even if it means laying down our life for them.

Development theories show how human beings normally progress through stages in order to reach the goal of being a well-integrated, self-actualized human being. Robert Roberts notes that a Christian psychology would emphasize "the need to stand in a relationship of mutual dependency and harmony with other human beings; and the need to take care of the creation."[295] He argues that psychological theories provide a description of human nature that not only explains who we are but where we are going. For those who do not accomplish the necessary developmental tasks, there are various strategies of therapy for 'fixing' what went wrong.

Evolutionary explanations of religion

If the brain evolved by natural selection, even the capacities to select particular esthetic judgments and religious beliefs must have arisen by the same mechanistic process.
E. O. Wilson

Why are we the way we are? Science attempts to explain human behaviour all the way from individual traits to the way we form together in societies and the moral impulses and ethical codes displayed in those communities. Daniel Dennett argues that religion is a cultural system that evolved as a survival mechanism for human beings in a hostile environment. He proposes that

---

[295] Robert Roberts, "Parameters of a Christian Psychology" in Robert C. Roberts and Mark R. Talbot, eds., *Limning the Psyche* (Grand Rapids, MI: W.B. Eerdmans, 1997), 77.

> the human mind is something of a bag of tricks, cobbled together over the eons by the foresightless prospect of evolution by natural selection. Driven by the demands of a dangerous world, it is deeply biased in favor of noticing the things that mattered most to the reproductive success of our ancestors.[296]

He interprets many characteristics of religion as cognitive traits that were once useful (eg. personifying inanimate objects) but took on a life of their own (making natural phenomena into gods) in a way that became detrimental to the individual (especially by giving the person a false view of their environment).

For example, in discussing fairy stories, he suggests that sometimes "fairy tales make up for not being true stories by having a moral which gives them an apparent value."[297] Why does he call the moral of the story an "apparent" value? Surely there are some real benefits to the practical advice extrapolated from such stories (for example, "look before you leap"). In addition, he sets aside the pure enjoyment of listening to a narrative to see how it unfolds (and to see our place in it).

Recently, the so-called "new atheists" have argued that religious belief is not only nonsensical but also harmful to societies.[298] Religious language sounds silly to many, with its seemingly outdated metaphysics of supernatural substances. Religion uses the everyday process of thinking to build up imaginative structures of meaning. Scott Atran defines religion in the following way: "Religion involves extraordinary use of ordinary cognitive processes to passionately display costly devotion to counter-intuitive worlds governed by spiritual

---

[296] Daniel Dennett, *Breaking the Spell: Religion as a Natural Phenomenon* (Penguin, 2006), 107.
[297] Ibid., 124.
[298] Richard Dawkins, *The God Delusion* (Houghton Mifflin, 2006).

agents."[299] He argues that "All religions follow the same structural contours. They invoke supernatural agents to deal with emotionally eruptive existential anxieties."[300] He sees a function for religions although the attribution of cause and effect is mistaken.

Pascal Boyer gives a similar account for the evolutionary development of religion. He argues that "at all times and all the time, indefinitely many variants of religious notions were and are created inside individual minds. Not all the variants are equally successful in cultural transmission."[301] Thus, religious ideas are memes (a concept Dawkins pioneered). They are mental dispositions copied with distortion (even in individual minds) by analogy with genes. A meme is a cultural product that is replicated in society.

Some of the mental modules that may be involved in religious explanations include inference engines (cause and effect reasoning) and agent detection.[302] Justin Barrett describes agent detection in this way: "Better to guess that the sound in the bushes is an agent (such as a person or a tiger) than assume it isn't and become lunch."[303] Barrett invokes the common theory of mind: "we have a tendency to invoke social or intentional causes when obvious mechanical or biological causes appear insufficient or absent."[304] This tendency is extrapolated to the ultimate explanation for everything that is (hence, intelligent design).

---

[299] Scott Atran, *In Gods we Trust: The Evolutionary Landscape of Religion* (Oxford University Press, 2002), 51.
[300] Scott Atran, "The Cognitive and Evolutionary Roots of Religion" in Patrick McNamara ed., *Where God and Science Meet* V.1 (Praeger Publishers, 2006), 201.
[301] Pascal Boyer, *Religion Explained: The Evolutionary Origins of Religious Thought* (Basic Books, 2001), 33.
[302] Boyer, 144.
[303] Justin Barrett, "Gods" in Harvey Whitehouse and James Laidlaw, *Religion, Anthropology and Cognitive Science* (Carolina Academic Press, 2007), 189.
[304] Ibid., 193.

The concept of a god is "minimally counterintuitive" since it piggybacks on the ordinary concepts we use to understand the world (eg. a person) and adds a twist (a person-like figure with supernatural powers). Barrett argues that "By virtue of being minimally counterintuitive, god concepts transmit easily and retain general plausibility. By virtue of being agents, gods have tremendous inference potential."[305] The gods are used to explain why things happen in the world. Barrett argues that "belief in gods arises because of the natural functioning of completely normal tools working in common natural and social contexts."[306] Is the belief justified? He suggests that the human imagination has a propensity to extrapolate our experiences into a supernatural realm (like Freud's argument that religion is a projection of our natural world into a heavenly realm).

The evolution of morality

Two things fill me with wonder: the starry sky above and the moral law within.
Immanuel Kant

Man still bears in his bodily frame the indelible stamp of his lowly origin.
Charles Darwin

Darwin's theory gravitated into the cultural realm when Herbert Spencer argued that even in our sophisticated societies the laws of nature prevail: compete and the fittest will survive (this so-called social Darwinism was at times used to justify the crudest forms of unrestrained capitalism). T. H. Huxley argued that a human being is

---

[305] Ibid., 203.
[306] Ibid., 21.

indebted to those qualities which he shares with the ape and the tiger; his exceptional physical organization; his cunning, his sociability, his curiosity, and his imitativeness; his ruthless and ferocious destructiveness when his anger is roused by opposition.[307]

Huxley concludes that human beings must transcend their animal nature in order to be ethical.

Many animal behaviours are actually selfish although they may look cooperative. Matt Ridley puts this view succinctly: "From the gene's point of view, therefore, the astonishing altruism of the worker ant was purely, unambiguously selfish."[308] In non-zero-sum games there are mutual benefits to be gained (because there is no winner). An example is the classic prisoner's dilemma, which if only played once, encourages both participants to act in self-interest. But if the game is played over and over again, Ridley argues, "Cooperation can, it seems, evolve spontaneously."[309] The best strategy is called Tit-for-tat, in which one mimics the move made by the other player.

Richard Dawkins argues that such behaviour is actually selfish since it benefits the genes of the acting entity. He suggests that

> individuals can be thought of as life-insurance underwriters. An individual can be expected to invest or risk a certain proportion of his own assets in the life of another individual. He takes into account his relatedness to the other individual, and also whether the individual is a 'good risk' in terms of his life expectancy compared with the insurer's own.[310]

---

[307] T. H. Huxley, "Evolution and Ethics," Romanes Lectures 1893. http://aleph0.clarku.edu/huxley/CE9/E-E.html
[308] Matt Ridley, *The Origins of Virtue* (Viking, 1996), 18.
[309] Ibid., 80.
[310] Dawkins, *The Selfish Gene*, 95.

In other words, the behaviour of an organism can be explained as a strategy to perpetuate its genetic heritage. Sometimes helping another organism with similar genes is an effective means to this end.

However, our genes do not determine our behaviour. Dawkins acknowledges that "Our genes may instruct us to be selfish, but we are not necessarily compelled to obey them all our lives. It may just be more difficult to learn altruism than it would be if we were genetically programmed to be altruistic."[311] On the other hand, violence would seem to be as natural as generosity. Frans de Waal says that "we descend ... from highly social mammals that know trust, loyalty and solidarity… [but] our evolutionary background makes it hard to identify with outsiders."[312] For example, chimpanzees engage in violence against others of their own species.

A cycle of virtue can result if both sides forsake self-interest. Arthur Peacocke argues that "humanity could have survived and flourished only if it had social and personal values that transcended the urges of the individual, embodying 'selfish' genes."[313] Cooperation increases the chance of survival (so it is naturally selected). Kenneth Miller thinks that

> Darwinian evolution can produce cooperation and care just as surely as conflict and competition. The care and self-sacrifice seen in animal families are not exceptions to evolution—rather, they are the straightforward results of natural selection acting to favor instinctive altruism.[314]

---

[311] Dawkins, *The Selfish Gene*, 3.
[312] Frans de Waal, "The Empathic Ape," *New Scientist* (Oct. 2005), 54.
[313] Arthur Peacocke, "Biology and a Theology of Evolution" in William Sweet and Richard Feist, eds. *Religion and the Challenges of Science* (Ashgate, 2007), 78.
[314] Miller, 248.

The amazing creativity of life-forms to interact symbiotically witnesses to the interconnected web of life that as a whole triumphs over death.

Human nature is (at least in part) cooperative and evolution has produced moral behaviours. Harold Broom gives an admirable summary of the new view:

> Moral attitudes (and structures within animals which make them possible) have not persisted by chance but because those individuals which had them gained selective advantage from having them. The basis for this is that certain genes would promote moral acts and those genes which interact with the environment to produce beneficial characters in the phenotype of the animal are more likely to persist in the population.[315]

Many behaviours fit the bill: cooperative strategies for hunting food, nurturing offspring, and even sacrifice for other individuals. Ian Barbour notes that "ants will sacrifice themselves to protect the colony."[316] This kind of extraordinary behaviour is rare, compared to the ordinary sacrifices that organisms make for others within their species.

Altruism carries some cost initially but is offset by the hope of a return favour.[317] Frans de Waal remarks: "Aiding others at a cost or risk to oneself is widespread in the animal world. The warning calls of birds allow other birds to escape a predator's talons but attract attention to the caller."[318] Broom restricts discussion of altruism to behaviours that require some cost, rather than cooperative actions (like hunting together) that

---

[315] Harold M. Broom, *The Evolution of Morality and Religion* (Cambridge University Press, 2003), 22-3.
[316] Ian Barbour, *Religion and Science: Historical and Contemporary Issues* (HarperSanFrancisco, 1997), 255.
[317] Broom, 36.
[318] Frans de Waal, *Good Natured: The Origins of Right and Wrong in Humans and other Animals* (Harvard University Press, 1996), 12.

enhance the chance of success for all (although perhaps at some risk if this means going after bigger game).

Broom identifies many cooperative behaviours which benefit individual organisms: feeding together, protecting the weaker members of the group, care for the young. This is the ordinary practical morality of sacrificing your own pleasure for the good of your family or your society, that Kantian duty which recognizes the universality of obligation (which has the happy byproduct of making the world a better place). Larry Arnhart argues:

> Natural selection favors not only kinship but also mutuality and reciprocity as grounds for cooperation and morality. Animals with the sociality and intelligence of human beings recognize that social cooperation can be mutually beneficial for all participants.[319]

One might see evolution promoting a subjective sense of 'ought' that generally raises the probability of successful transmission of genes similar to the individuals (this is sometimes called 'group selection,' but the idea that natural selection operates at the level of the group is a controversial notion).

Some behaviours which many societies consider immoral may also be a result of natural selection. The male of a species, for example, would benefit by breeding with as many females as possible in order to ensure many children. However, for a female, a long courtship ensures that children are your own. Since the female is in demand, it is to her advantage to refuse to copulate, to ensure that the male commits. Note the social side of the equation (explanation at a higher level): what is the pay-off for restrictive sexual moralities? Or on the other side, what happens to a society that permits sexual liberties? Do morals sometimes go against nature?

---

[319] Larry Arnhart, "The Darwinian Moral Sense and Biblical religion" in Philip Clayton and Jeffrey Schloss, eds. *Evolution and Ethics: Human Morality in Biological and Religious Perspectives* (Eerdman's. 2004), 209.

Even if behaviour is rooted in our biological nature, there is still a difference between our drives and our ethical decisions. Frans de Waal puts it this way:

> Biologists may tell us how things are, perhaps even analyze human nature in intricate detail, yet there is no logical connection between the typical form and frequency of a behaviour (a statistical measure of what is 'normal') and the value we attach to it (a moral decision).[320]

The sociobiological explanations of ethics fall victim to the naturalistic fallacy (the failure to distinguish between the 'is' and the 'ought').

On the other hand, ethics must be rooted in what human beings actually can do (Kant's dictum: ought implies can). Francisco Ayala argues that

> humans are ethical by their biological nature. Humans evaluate their behaviour as right or wrong, moral or immoral, as a consequence of their eminent intellectual capacities, which include self-awareness and abstract thinking.[321]

What are the ethical standards that should be followed given those capacities? That is a philosophical question, not a scientific one.

It would make sense for religion to develop as a social system based upon the biological capacities of the human organism. E. O. Wilson recognizes that religion plays a powerful and beneficial role in society. He acknowledges:

> In the midst of the chaotic and potentially disorienting experiences each person undergoes daily, religion classifies him, provides him with unquestioned membership in a group claiming great powers, and by

---

[320] De Waal, 38.
[321] Francisco Ayala, "Biology to Ethics: An Evolutionist's View of Human Nature" in Giovanni Boniolo and Gabriele de Anna, eds., *Evolutionary Ethics and Contemporary Biology* (Cambridge University Press, 2006), 148.

this means gives him a driving purpose in life compatible with his self-interest.[322]

Nevertheless, Wilson argues that we should replace the old worn-out myths of the great religions with a scientific myth (the evolutionary epic). He realizes that science does not have the emotional power of religion, but suggests that marrying science and art might yield a cultural artifact of great power.

Religions remind us that we are a unitary person, not a body-soul dualism. Similarly, science can show us that we are a creature, but unique among animals. We are not totally determined by our genes. The monotheistic religions emphasize that we are created in God's image, but fallen: capable of good and evil. All religions aim to develop the whole human being. Religious rituals are in many ways aimed at transfiguring us into a new creation.

---

[322] E. O. Wilson, *On Human Nature* (Harvard University Press, 1978), 188.

Ecological considerations

How long will the land lie parched
and the grass in every field be withered?
Because those who live in it are wicked,
the animals and birds have perished.
Moreover, the people are saying,
"He will not see what happens to us."
Jeremiah 12:4

A human being is a part of a whole, called by us
'universe', a part limited in time and space. He
experiences himself, his thoughts and feelings as
something separated from the rest... a kind of optical
delusion of his consciousness. This delusion is a kind of
prison for us, restricting us to our personal desires and
to affection for a few persons nearest to us. Our task
must be to free ourselves from this prison by widening
our circle of compassion to embrace all living creatures
and the whole of nature in its beauty.
Albert Einstein

The study of the processes of life does not only involve questions about origins, but also the study of the complex systems operating within the natural world. Human life is enmeshed in a web of interactions with animals and plants, as well as the material elements necessary for life, such as water and air. Theologians have been quick to adopt the impulses of the environmental movement. There are, of course, major ethical concerns which are raised about human responsibility for the care of the earth. Christian thinkers have been forced to respond to this issue since Christianity itself has been accused of being partly responsible for a human attitude of 'dominion' over nature. Lynn White, Jr., dramatically argued that Christianity is responsible for the state we are in. He suggests that the text in Genesis 1:28, where God says "fill the earth and subdue it. / Rule over the fish of the sea and the birds of the air and over every living creature that moves on the ground" has given license for Christians to dominate the natural world. A more accurate interpretation would say that human beings are supposed to take care of God's creation (this is the principle of stewardship).

As well, White argues that Christianity established a "dualism of man and nature but also insisted that it is God's will that man exploit nature for his proper ends."[323] Human beings are created in the image of God, it is true, and that gives us not only special status but also special responsibility. We are the ones who are free to pollute our environment (so much that it may return on us the fruits of our sins). The Christian solution is not to separate human beings from the rest of creation or even to elevate us above the rest of nature but to focus on our responsibility for our environment.

Hindu theology has also been accused of anthropocentrism. The Advaita (non-dualistic) tradition emphasizes the oneness of all reality so much that everything is seen as spirit (Brahman). However, this oneness also promotes a vision of interconnectedness. The Bhagavad Gita personifies Brahman in the avatar of Krishna: "I am the taste in water, the brilliance in the moon and sun, the sacred syllable (Om) in all the Vedas, the sound in air and virility in men" (*Bhagavad Gita* 7:8). Anantanand Rambachan interprets this to mean that "The

---

[323] Lynn White, Jr., *Machina ex Deo: Essays in the Dynamism of Western Culture* (Cambridge, MA: Massachusetts Institute of Technology Press, 1968), 86.

Advaita teaching about the fundamental ontological unicity of brahman, world and human beings is understood as promoting a reverence and value for nature that is conducive to sound environmental ethics." [324] Because the atman (the human self) is essentially one with Brahman in this Hindu way of thinking, we are so connected to the earth that its pain is ours!

As a solution within Christianity, White proposes Saint Francis of Assisi: "Francis tried to depose man from his monarchy over creation and set up a democracy of all God's creatures."[325] The beauty of Francis's sermon to the birds, though, is not a democratic evocation of equals, but a symbol of the complex inter-relationships between creatures of different abilities. Sallie McFague proposes to extend the traditional Christian model of God to better interact with our current scientific theories. She uses the imagery of birth to depict the act of creation: "The universe is bodied forth from God, it is expressive of God's being, it could, therefore, be seen as God's body."[326] If we think this way, she suggests, we would see ourselves as part of an interconnected universe deeply connected to its divine source.

Systems ecology and the divine

Praised be You my Lord with all Your creatures,
especially Sir Brother Sun,
Who is the day through whom You give us light.
And he is beautiful and radiant with great splendour,
Of You Most High, he bears the likeness.
Saint Francis of Assisi

---

[324] Anantanand Rambachan, *A Hindu theology of Liberation: Not-two is not One*. (Albany, NY: Suny Press, 2015), 132.
[325] White, 91.
[326] Sally McFague, "Models of God" in Russell, *Physics, Philosophy and Theology*, 259.

One impulse from a vernal wood
May teach you more of man,
Of moral evil and of good,
Than all the sages can.
William Wordsworth

The systems theories of ecology have been very influential in recent theology. Arthur Peacocke summarizes this tendency towards wholism:

> It is clear that the activities of the parts and the patterns they form are what they are *because* of their incorporation into the 'system-as-a-whole.' In fact, they are patterns within the system. ... The parts would not behave as observed if they were not parts of that particular system (the whole).[327]

All of this creative activity was put into the creation by God for a purpose. The Bible emphasizes this overarching concern towards people (it is rather sketchy, after all, on the physical details of how we came to be here; what matters is what we do in this existence). Peacocke rephrases the creation story: "There was God. And God was All-That-Was. God's Love overflowed and God said, 'Let Other be.'"[328] The creation was made by God in order to experience something different! Even more, God created out of love, since the inter-relationships within the divine being call forth the existence of something new (just as the love of parents for each other calls forth beings that are new and loved in their own identity).

The so-called "Gaia theory" posits that the planet as a whole can be seen as a self-regulating mechanism. James Lovelock argues that this view of the planet encourages us to take care of it: "Being curious and getting to know the natural

---

[327] Arthur Peacocke, *Paths from Science towards God*, 52.
[328] Ibid., 1.

world leads to a loving relationship with it."³²⁹ Like an organism, it assimilates energy, adapting within itself to prevent that influx from upsetting the balanced temperature range within which life survives. The planet takes care of us, by recycling waste products of some organisms as food for others (eg. We breathe out carbon dioxide which trees 'inhale'; otherwise the atmosphere would become toxic to us). However, he cautions: "In no way do I see Gaia as a sentient being, a surrogate God."³³⁰ We must be careful about assigning anthropomorphic images—it is inappropriate to assign human purposive activity to a functional system (the parts of which are playing a purpose, but only as a part of an interacting network).

Ursula Goodenough sees a spiritual energy working within matter. She paints a vivid picture of life and its complexities:

> Our story tells us of the sacredness of life, of the astonishing complexity of cells and organisms, of the vast lengths of time it took to generate their splendid diversity, of the enormous improbability that any of it happened at all. Reverence is the religious emotion elicited when we perceive the sacred. We are called to revere the whole enterprise of planetary existence, the whole and all of its myriad parts as they catalyze and secrete and replicate and mutate and evolve.³³¹

It would be more theologically accurate to say that we should revere the source of this sacred existence. Goodenough rejects a transcendental cause for the beauty of nature:

> For me, the existence of all this complexity and awareness and intent and beauty, and my ability to apprehend it, serves as the ultimate meaning and the ultimate value. The continuation of life reaches around,

---

[329] James Lovelock, *The Ages of Gaia: A Biography of our Living Earth* (Norton, 1988), 194.
[330] Lovelock, 204.
[331] Goodenough, 170.

> grabs its own tail, and forms a sacred circle that requires no further justification, no Creator, no superordinate meaning of meaning, no purpose other than that the continuation continue until the sun collapses or the final meteor collides. I confess a credo of continuation.[332]

It is not enough, though, to simply preserve the balance of nature as it is. The theory of evolution shows that the equilibrium of nature can change. Human beings now have the capacity to intervene in nature in quite dramatic ways. We should of course be careful about this but there is no divine necessity that simply insists that nature be left alone. This is the paradox of stewardship: we are called to take care of nature and move it forward in some sense.

Some theologians, such as Thomas Berry, have proclaimed a new version of the creation story, given our current scientific knowledge of where we came from. This story emphasizes the immense time-frame after the "first three minutes" (as Steven Weinberg describes the seminal moments of the Big Bang) as the forces of nature worked out the possibilities within themselves. This story gives glory to God for the wise development of the cosmos according to natural laws that generate self-organizing systems, including life itself. We should celebrate the constant impetus of creative emergence of new forms, even the dramatic 'quantum leap' of consciousness, arising from the neuronal interaction within our brains.

Diarmuid O'Murchu writes a new creed that spells out the theological implications of the "new scientific creation story:"

> I believe in the creative energy of the divine, erupting with unimaginable exuberance, transforming the seething vacuum into a whirlwind of zest and flow.

---

[332] Ibid., 171.

> I believe in the divine imprint as it manifests itself in swirling vortexes and particle formations, birthing forth atoms and galaxies.
>
> I believe in the providential outburst of supernovas and in the absorbing potential of black holes.[333]

In a provocative explanation of this concept, Brian Swimme (who co-authored *The Universe Story* with Thomas Berry) explains the radical implications of this new scientific understanding of reality. He calls the universe a "green dragon" in order to emphasize the inadequate metaphorical nature of our language.[334] We don't understand the universe sufficiently, but what we do know through science gives us a 'big picture' that should help us to understand our role in the universe. He argues that this empirical 'creation myth' will help us come to a proper relationship with our environment.

Green religion

Creating God, your fingers trace
the bold designs of farthest space.
Let sun and moon and stars and light
and what lies hidden praise your might.

Sustaining God, your hands uphold
earth's myst'ries known or yet untold.
Let water's fragile blend with air,
enabling life, proclaim your care.
  Jeffery W. Rowthorn

Christians often use the word 'creation' to distinguish this reality from the scientific view, which tends to think of nature as an independent entity, explained without reference to God.

---

[333] Diarmuid O'Murchu, *Evolutionary Faith* (Orbis Books, 2002), 3.
[334] Brian Swimme, "The Universe is a Green Dragon: Reading the Meaning in the Cosmic Story." http://www.context.org/ICLIB/IC12/Swimme.htm

Metropolitan Paulos Mar Gregorios, former President of the World Council of Churches, details a Christian theory of nature. When thinking about creation, he argues that there are nuances within this concept: first, God is uncreated and creating (the source of all that is); second, the cosmos is created but also creating in the sense that it continues the work of God's primary act; third, humans are created and not creating (most moderns think of human conscious invention as the primary cause of creativity!); and fourth, the final restoration of the world (the new heaven and the new earth) will be uncreated and not creating. [335] This multi-level analysis of creation introduces a larger context for understanding (especially God as a source of explanation). It holds together God, humanity and the cosmos, and emphasizes the relations between them.

Wendell Berry, a Christian ecologist who lives on a farm in Kentucky, gives one of the best explanations of the way in which Christianity poses a larger context in which all things "live and move and have [their] being" (Acts 17:28). The biosphere, with all of its inter-connecting cycles and systems, proclaims the goodness of God in its order. Berry says that "everything in the Kingdom of God is joined both to it and to everything else that is in it; that is to say, the Kingdom of God is orderly."[336] Berry calls this larger context the "Great Economy," a less religiously-packed term than its Biblical name, the Kingdom of God.

We are charged to conserve and protect our home, but not only because it benefits us (notice how much of the rhetoric from the environmental movement is anthropocentric—don't pollute because it will harm you!). Berry argues: "A good human economy, that is, defines and values human goods, and, like the Great Economy, it conserves and protects its goods. It proposes

---

[335] Metropolitan Paulos Mar Gregorios, "A Theory of Nature: An Introduction." http://www.goarch.org/ourfaith/ourfaith8045
[336] Wendell Berry, *Home Economics* (North Point Press, 1987), 55.

to endure."[337] Creation, seen from a Christian perspective, is a gift from God, and so must be treasured in itself. It derives its intrinsic worth from its ultimate source. We should care about the environment because we are in intimate relationship with every part of nature, and we should exhibit God's love to nature. Wendell Berry argues that "everything in the Kingdom of God is joined both to it and to everything else that is in it."[338] This approach is like the Buddhist conception that when we harm the environment we harm ourselves (polluting the rivers is literally dumping poison into our blood).

      Christians believe that God created a good earth but that it is broken by the presence of sin. Human beings in their freedom can fall into selfishness and forget about our responsibility for others (even other things). The ideal, Berry proposes, is a "maximum of well-being with the minimum of consumption."[339] We are a part of God's creation, and participate in its suffering and its joy. We should, in fact, work to make the environment glorify God by fulfilling its existence (the water should shout clear praise to God). John Haught sees nature as a window to the divine nature: "A sacrament is anything which we are gifted with a sense of the sacred, and it is especially nature's beauty and vitality that have communicated to humans an impression of the divine."[340] If nature is sacred (but not divine) then we will love it for what it is and for what it should be: a reflection of God's being (or a physical refraction of the spiritual).

---

[337] Ibid., 60.
[338] Ibid., 55.
[339] Ibid., 72.
[340] John Haught, "Theology and Ecology in an Unfinished Universe" in David Lodge and Christopher Hamlin, eds. *Religion and the New Ecology: Environmental Responsibility in a World of Flux* (University of Notre Dame Press, 2006), 233.

Spirit in the world

You, my God, are the inmost depths, the stability of that eternal milieu, *without duration or space, in which our cosmos emerges gradually into being and grows gradually to its final completeness, as it loses those boundaries which to our eyes seem so immense.*
Teilhard de Chardin

Do not feel lonely, the entire universe is inside you.
Rumi

Some ecological views yield a more radical conclusion: that God is everywhere (pantheism) or that everything is in God (panentheism). Niels Henrik Gregersen puts it this way:
> Understanding all things to be in God, as it were, means that we can be at home with God anywhere in the universe. The logic of infinity permits us to think of the presence of God in the midst of reality—without replacing the finite with the infinite. Since there exists no matter without God being present in it, we have the interesting formulas: *God + nature = nature* while *nature - God = 0.*[341]

The second equation, if manipulated by taking God to the other side, seems to resolve into pantheism: God = nature. The first equation, by performing a similar manipulation, is resolvable to the following paradox: God = 0! These are philosophical equations rather than mathematical, but I think that their simple algebraic manipulation does reveal some logical problems.

Ruth Page proposes that we see everything 'with' God rather than 'in' God. She proposes a modified position which she calls pansynthesism: "any extension of panentheism to the

---

[341] Niels Henrik Gregersen, "Three Varieties of Panentheism" in Clayton and Peacocke, 35.

proposition that God is 'in' creatures, human or nonhuman, is questionable. A relationship is close, but not so close that one is overwhelmed by the other."[342] This avoids a pantheism of identifying God with the forces of nature but acknowledges that God acts through those forces. What good is this supernatural force added to the natural force? Does Occam's razor force us to slice away unnecessary entities in our explanation? What is the cash value of God's action in nature?

An awareness of the universe story will help us remember our place in the 'great chain of being.' We are set in the midst of this great cosmic dance and we are not able to influence the fundamental constituents of the universe. This should help us overcome our hubris, but it also should help us to connect with the ground of our being, the creator of this grand show. Annie Dillard says it poetically: "everywhere I look I see fire; that which isn't flint is tinder, and the whole world sparks and flames."[343] All of creation is burning with the passion of God, right from the very start. Our appreciation of God's work must begin with a realization that, in Gerard Manley Hopkins' words, "The world is charged with the grandeur of God. / It will flame out, like shining from shook foil."[344] We need to look at nature in order to catch glimpses of the reality of God shining through the cracks in the cosmos.

Buddhism is often touted as the most 'green' religion because it encourages us to connect with everything around us. There's a joke about a Buddhist who goes into Harvey's and they ask him what he wants on his burger. He says: "Make me one with everything." Donald Swearer suggests that "Buddhist environmentalists find in the causal principle of interdependence an ecological vision that integrates all aspects of the ecosphere—

---

[342] Ruth Page, "Panentheism and Pansynthesism: God in Relation" in Clayton and Peacocke, 231.
[343] Annie Dillard, *Pilgrim at Tinker Creek* (Bantam Books, 1975), 10.
[344] Gerard Manley Hopkins, "God's Grandeur"
http://www.poetryfoundation.org/poems-and-poets/poems/detail/44395

particular individuals and general species—in terms of the principle of mutual codependence."[345] The current Dalai Lama says it this way: "The world grows smaller and smaller, more and more interdependent."[346] In Buddhism, meditation is sometimes used as the practice of compassion for others and everything around us.

---

[345] Donald K. Swearer, "Buddhism and Ecology: Challenge and Promise" *Earth Ethics* 10, no.1 (Fall 1998).
[346] http://www.arcworld.org/faiths.asp?pageID=129

Stories of salvation

Reason, that proceeds from God, that is implanted in all from the beginning and is the first law in us and is bound up in all, leads us up to God through visible things.
Gregory Nazianzus, *Theological orations*

While it is difficult to bridge the "two cultures" of science and faith (to borrow an image from C. P. Snow, comparing the sciences and the humanities[347]), there are important metaphorical images that cross over the gap between these two mental disciplines. I advocate an intersectional method: theology and science together are needed in order to adequately describe reality. They are two different perspectives on the same world, but they need to be compared in order for their full contribution to be realized. They are like our eyes: two standpoints are necessary in order for us to achieve depth of vision.[348] This last section will focus on Christian ideas that can help make sense of our scientific reality.

---

[347] C. P. Snow, *The Two Cultures* (London; New York: Cambridge University Press, 1993).
[348] See Northrop Frye, *The Double Vision: Language and Meaning in Religion* (University of Toronto Press, 1991) for this idea applied to the dialogue between literature and theology.

In many ways, we live our lives according to the stories we tell each other and ourselves. Narratives about our families, our nation, and our world give meaning to our daily existence. Stories shape us in unaccountable ways, giving us direction as we struggle to understand our lives. In our contemporary culture, there are many stories to choose from: the myth of progress, the epic of self-fulfillment, the legend of the quest for certainty. Religious stories compete with other histories of salvation: political, economic, and technological.

The Christian story of salvation is set within the history of God's action in the world. We can see the structure of this story (the plot of the Christian narrative) in the Apostles' Creed. It begins: "I believe in God the Father, maker of heaven and earth," and proceeds to highlight the essentials of the faith, through to the resurrection of the dead. The grand sweep of that narrative runs from creation through the fall of human beings, their redemption, and to the end of the universe (and time itself!). Christians interpret history through the lens of this story, which is a summary of the broad sweep of the Biblical records.[349] We should not interpret the creeds like a scientific textbook. They are a different literary genre, a different way of telling the story of the universe.

Gregg Easterbrook acknowledges the common view of the scientific story: "Science was assumed to be in the process of generating hard evidence that life is just replicating molecules and vibrating atoms, signifying nothing."[350] Science seems to be telling a different story today: "the leading theory of the Big Bang, called 'inflation' physics, holds that cogent physical laws were at work during the genesis; that entire galaxies can spring forth from microscopic pinpoints of seemingly empty space."[351]

---

[349] See John Honner, "Cosmology and the Creed" *Compass* 14 (Sept./Oct. 1993).
[350] Gregg Easterbrook, "Meaning Makes a Comeback," in Stannard, 32.
[351] Ibid., 33.

The scientific framework is used in a religious way when it provides an overall understanding of reality.

Easterbrook argues that science is now saying that the universe is conducive to the formation of life: "the basic rules of chemistry, thermodynamics, and even mathematics have been ordered in ways that encourage both life and consciousness."[352] Today the scientific myth shows that "humanity is part of some larger, greater, and perhaps welcoming cosmic enterprise."[353] It sounds more like Mother Nature than God!

Science is a beautiful way of perceiving the world. Mary Midgley argues that science and religion have the same cognitive source: "both are rooted in a sense of wonder." Then, when science is finished, "serious scientists experience a sense of awe."[354] Science represents progress not only in knowledge, but also in human appreciation of the world. Midgeley claims: "They have changed our imaginative picture of the world. They have shown us how to look at the facts differently so that the picture makes more sense."[355] Science notes the complex order which is found everywhere in creation.

This response can be seen as evidence in favour of the spiritual character of human beings, if not the universe itself. John Polkinghorne argues that "Scientists habitually experience wonder at the beauty of the physical world, and this is a kind of prayer."[356] However, it is one thing to experience awe, and another to pray to a personal creator. He argues that "divine action will always be hidden, for it will be contained within the cloudiness of unpredictable processes."[357] Thus, prayer can be seen as effective today because we don't know all the variables.

---

[352] Ibid., 33.
[353] Ibid., 34.
[354] Mary Midgley, "The Need for Wonder" in Stannard, 186.
[355] Ibid., 188.
[356] Polkinghorne, *Quarks, Chaos and Christianity* (Crossroad, 1996), 62.
[357] Ibid., 72.

Theology is a broader discipline than science, attempting to synthesize all of our thinking and feeling. Alister McGrath argues that natural theology is an illumination of the doctrines of Christian faith: it is

> not about discovering persuasive grounds of faith outside the bounds and scope of revelation, but a demonstration that when nature is 'seen' through the lens of the Christian revelation, the outcome is imaginatively compelling and rationally persuasive.[358]

Religion places that thinking in the midst of experience and action using creative and artistic forms.

Intersection

Science can purify religion from error and superstition. Religion can purify science from idolatry and false absolutes.
Pope John Paul II

Some religious approaches to science see it as an exclusive relation. In this traditional conflict model one has to choose: either one is true or the other. This approach has been taken in fundamentalist versions of religion that rely on a literal interpretation of scriptures. Another approach is the inclusive approach. Both science and religion are seen as valid understandings but different. This idea is popular because it gives identifiable roles for the two practices (eg. fact and meaning). I propose another model: the "intersectional" approach. My approach does not separate the two disciplines according to function. Instead, the comparisons between religious and scientific ideas are noted based on their metaphorical power. It matters how we see the world, but we do

---

[358] Alister McGrath, *The Order of Things: Explorations in Scientific Theology* (Blackwell, 2006), 68.

so with lenses fashioned by the shape of our theories. I call this "synthetic" theology instead of using the traditional word "systematic." Theology today should combine the approaches of intersecting disciplines.

Pope John Paul II has given some marvelous guidance to the religion-science dialogue. He argues that thought must "move from *phenomenon* to *foundation* ... speculative thinking must penetrate to the spiritual core and the ground from which it rises." He notes that "scientists discover the laws which govern the universe, as well as their interrelationship. They stand in wonderment and humility before the created order." He says that "God loves to make himself heard in the silence of creation."[359] The book of nature is more difficult to 'read' than the book of revelation because it does not speak.

Thus, John Paul II blessed the work of scientists: "research, by exploring the greatest and the smallest, contributes to the glory of God which is reflected in every part of the universe." However, science should always be put in service to the human person. He says to scientists: "You are asked to work in a way that serves the good of individuals and of all humanity, while always being attentive to the dignity of every human being and to respect for creation."[360] Scientists have an ethical obligation not only to use their knowledge responsibly, but to go about research responsibly (choosing which areas are fruitful, being honest about the data).

Theology used to be called the "queen of the sciences." The Latin word *'scientia'* meant knowledge but I don't think we can see theology any longer as a science, at least in the modern experimental sense. Although empirical data are important for measuring the validity of theological statements, theological statements should not be seen as hypotheses. Instead, theology is

---

[359] Pope John Paul II, "Address, Jubilee of Scientists" (May 25, 2000). http://www.cin.org/pope/jubilee-scientists.html
[360] Pope John Paul II.

one of the humanities, and should be seen by analogy with philosophy rather than a science devoted to a materialist method. Theology is an inquiry into the ideas that ground our view of nature. They are meta-natural propositions about the conditions for nature rather than propositions about the structure of nature.

In a way, theology proposes hypotheses that can be tested empirically. Nancey Murphy proposes that theology be seen as similar to a scientific research program. She argues that a progressive research program results in "greater demonstrated ability to anticipate novel facts"[361] and discusses several cases of Christian doctrines that can be measured by such a process. She focuses on historical propositions, especially practical ones such as ethics and ecclesiology.

Of course theology as an academic discipline is a research program but is it finding anything new? Theologians offer opinions about how to view the whole of human reality (especially our relation to God, our human status, and the possible and desired directions of history). Empirical data is important in judging these views, especially historical data about how human beings have thought and acted throughout the centuries. Scientific theories are important as constraints upon possible theological views of the universe. Theology is like the arts (especially literature) in that it includes the affective response to the human situation in the cosmos. It seeks to give meaning to the scientific descriptions of human being, given that we are beings able to reflect not only upon what we are but upon what we should be. Theology is also creative in that it is an individual interpretation.

The modern ecumenical movement has settled on the formula that every denomination of the Christian church has a unique gift to offer. There are some general theological principles we can all agree upon, but they are not the sort of

---

[361] Nancey Murphy, *Theology in the Age of Scientific Reasoning* (Cornell University Press, 1990), 61.

empirical propositions that science is able to test. First of all, they are metaphysical statements. That is to say, they summarize what must be true in general about the nature of reality (and, having nothing other than reality to observe, we cannot run experiments on that statement). Second, they are about realities that have an unobservable dimension (especially the God that transcends our physical and material being).

What would an experimental theological research program look like? Alister McGrath claims that in a scientific theology "the church is the observatory."[362] Should we propose empirical studies that can be done in the ecclesial laboratories scattered throughout the world? My own tradition, Anabaptist theology, proposes one possibility. The emphasis of the Radical Reformers on discipleship makes theology empirical (eg. Hans Denck: "no one may truly know Christ except one who follows him in life").[363] The process of discernment by the community is like the method of peer review, although it would look more like the process in the humanities: cumulative analysis of the tradition of texts in collaboration with the experiences of people throughout human history. Nonviolence, for example, can be seen as an experiment in resistance against evil.

Wisdom's manifestation: Sophia

There is in all visible things an invisible fecundity, a dimmed light, a meek namelessness, a hidden wholeness. ... There is in all things an inexhaustible sweetness and purity, a silence that is a fount of action and joy. It rises up in word-less gentleness and flows out to me from the unseen roots of all created being, welcoming me tenderly, saluting me with indescribable humility. This is at once my own being, my own nature,

---

[362] McGrath, *The Order of Things*, 218.
[363] http://gameo.org/index.php?title=Denck,_Hans_(ca._1500-1527)

and the Gift of my Creator's Thought and Art within me, speaking as Hagia Sophia, speaking as my sister, Wisdom.
Thomas Merton, "Hagia Sophia"

Does nature give us knowledge of God? Christians throughout the ages have attempted to derive some knowledge about God by looking at nature. In Romans 1, Paul says that God's "eternal power and divine nature" can be seen by looking at nature. This knowledge is accessible to all, through their natural power of reason, contemplating the nature around it (and penetrating into its fundamental nature). Furthermore, if this is true, it would explain how God's grace can be available to those who have not had access to special revelation (the story of Christ).

God sustains the creation by upholding the very laws that make it function. William Stoeger proposes "that everything that happens can be explained by the processes, regularities, and interrelationships described by physics, chemistry and biology."[364] However, this should not cause the Christian to lose faith. Rather, we should realize that "God acts not in supposed gaps in the laws of nature, but rather in and through the laws themselves. They are expressions of God's creative activity in nature."[365] This formulation expresses the Christian doctrine of providence (God keeps the universe running on its course).

In the twentieth century, the Swiss theologian Karl Barth argued vociferously against any natural theology. In his view, our knowledge of God comes as a gift, and should not be built up from any general analysis of the structure of existence. Nevertheless, if God has created this world, it should then be possible to at least develop a 'theology of nature,' that is, an explanation of how our scientific knowledge correlates with what we know about God through the primary source (Christ).

---

[364] William Stoeger, "Can God Really Act in our Lives?" in Stannard, 166.
[365] Ibid., 167.

Even more than that, if nature is indeed created by God then we need to ask how the creation displays the handiwork of God. Many today argue that 'intelligent design' shows God's participation in the formation of nature. However, a more radical view of the design of nature would show that intelligence embedded within the structures of nature (for example, in the ability of matter to 'self-organize' into more and more complex systems).

Eastern Orthodox thinkers have proposed an intriguing model of God's relation to the world through the third person of the trinity. The spirit of God proceeds directly from God in Orthodox theology (rather than from the Father and the Son in the famous *'filioque'* phrase of the Western version of the Nicene Creed). Of course, all three persons of the trinity act together (known as *'circumincessio'* or *'perichoresis'*), but Orthodox theology supports a closer link between the creative activity of God in the origin of the world and God's ongoing creative activity through the spirit (not only in human affairs but also in other parts of the natural world).

Sergei Bulgakov proposed that God is mediated to the creation through the figure of Sophia (God's wisdom), traditionally associated most closely with the spirit, the third person of the trinity. Although considered as heretical by some (since Sophia seems to take on a semi-divine nature almost making her a fourth person of the trinity), Bulgakov was clear that Sophia should be seen as a mediation of God's being in the creation, displaying God's reality somehow in this reality (not fully; perhaps obscured; always mysterious). Bulgakov puts it poetically: "Things and matter absorb the invisibly descending grace of the Holy Spirit the way the earth absorbs moisture."[366] If God truly acts in the universe today, something of God's divine purpose must be active in the structures of our existence (instead of thinking of God's actions as miracles that defy the

---

[366] Sergei Bulgakov, *The Comforter* (Eerdman's, 2004), 221.

order of nature, this proposal would allow us to see God working "with the grain of the universe").

The Christian model of God as Trinity has given some images by which to think about how God can create a world that is independent yet also displays some of the attributes of God. The first chapter of John is a hymn to the 'logos' which was present at creation ("In the beginning was the word" John 1:1). This passage is often seen as a 'midrash' (a rabbinic commentary) on Sophia (wisdom) as portrayed in Proverbs 8: 22-31 (NIV):

> The LORD brought me forth as the first of his works,
>   before his deeds of old;
> I was appointed from eternity,
>   from the beginning, before the world began....
> I was there when he set the heavens in place,
>   when he marked out the horizon on the face of the deep,
>   when he established the clouds above
>   and fixed securely the fountains of the deep.

The wisdom of God is portrayed in Proverbs and the prologue of John as an expression of God's being almost like Plato's demiurge which brings about the instantiation of the 'forms.' But in Christian thinking this aspect of God is identified with Jesus the Christ.[367] In Philippians, Christ is described as the 'form of God' that is incarnated in matter ("Who, being in very nature God, did not consider equality with God something to be grasped, made himself nothing, taking the very nature of a servant being made in human likeness." Philippians 2:7 NIV). God is revealed in human form (this is called 'special' revelation as opposed to the general revelation of God's being in nature).

---

[367] Celia Deane-Drummond gives a helpful overview of Christian reflection on the divine wisdom in *Creation through Wisdom: Theology and the New Biology* (T & T Clark, 2000).

Christian theology gives a unique answer to these age-old questions. God created a good world, distinct from the divine being, but with finite and very real existence. Human beings display the image of God, and have the capacity to relate to God, but are free to love God or to turn away and do evil. Why is science so challenging to Christians, then? If one's relation to God is purely personal then science has nothing to say about it. Nature itself displays something of the image of God as well. If it is created by God, then it is rationally ordered towards some end: a goal that God had in mind for it.

Religions must incorporate the current scientific picture of reality into their conception of what kind of world God created. Do we need to modify our theology based on these discoveries and theories? Our understanding of God is necessarily influenced by our knowledge of the physical basis of our existence. However, if God is the creator, he holds a 'transcendental trump card' in that God is the source of creation, and thus inscrutable to a certain extent, being so much greater than the creation. This is not to say that our intellectual striving is useless, only limited. Our ideas have some congruence with ultimate reality, but never a perfect correspondence.

Ways of seeing the universe

Science without religion is lame; religion without science is blind.
Albert Einstein

Many religions have seen the universe as created by God. Many Christian medieval manuscripts, as well as sculptures in cathedrals, contain images of God creating the universe. Michelangelo depicted God creating the sun, moon and earth (in the fresco in the Sistine chapel less famous than the creation of Adam). This image of a powerful deity creating our universe in all its immensity and intricacy gives an explanation for the order and complexity that we see displayed wherever we turn our eyes.

Science seems to have replaced this rather personal, intimate portrait of a god fashioning the world especially for us. This scientific age demands a different attitude towards life and the world than the traditional religious approach of faith. Many Christian theologians, however, have begun to integrate scientific discoveries and theories into their thinking about God, human beings, and the world. Can our study of nature reveal something about the "mind of God?" Instead of science being seen as an enemy of religion, is it instead a source of revelation (a 'book of works' instead of a 'book of words')?

Theology represents its ideas in creative forms (not only literary, but also in other artistic media). McGrath suggests that "On a Christian understanding of things, a truly natural theology appeals to the human imagination, not simply the human reason."[368] The cathedrals of the middle ages were 'sermons in stone:' the sculptures and stained glass windows portrayed the essential messages of the faith. Eastern Orthodox theologians like to say that theology is a form of prayer. It is 'living the questions' not only in the midst of the most significant experiences of life (celebrated in the church 'from womb to tomb') but also in the 'ordinary time' of reflective meditation between those intense 'peak experiences.'

The biblical concept of creation draws on the Jewish dedication to a powerful God actively interested in the formation and preservation of the universe. God speaks and the world comes into being. Unlike Greek rationalism, however, which aimed for the perfection of the ideal, Jewish notions of God emphasized the relatedness of God. Aristotle had proposed a "prime mover," a metaphysically different agent that grounds the reality of all that we see (the prime mover is thought itself, which for Aristotle was the most fundamental reality).

---

[368] McGrath, *The Order of Things* 96.

Aristotle's unmoved mover contemplated only pure thought (that is, itself). Matter was unworthy of consideration. In contrast, the wisdom tradition gives a rather personal depiction of the work of God.

The author of the apocryphal book of Sirach (also called Ecclesiasticus), written less than 200 years before the birth of Christ, gives an account of the creation. He begins with a hymn to the rational order of the cosmos:

> When the Lord created his works from the beginning,
>   and, in making them, determined their boundaries,
> he arranged his works in an eternal order,
>   and their dominion for all generations.
> (Sirach 16: 26-27a)

The creation itself is depicted in somewhat anthropomorphic terms, giving it an agency in itself:

> They neither hunger nor grow weary,
>   and they do not abandon their tasks.
> They do not crowd one another,
>   and they never disobey his word.
> (Sirach 16: 27b-28)

It is easy to see that the world is governed by laws that can be intelligently formulated with our most precise mathematical tools. However, creation is not simply the outgrowth of a purely rational mind, intent on inventing a system (like a computer game designer).

Creation as order

Necessity is God's veil. God has committed all phenomena without exception to the mechanism of the world.
Simone Weil

The wind has settled, the blossoms have fallen;
Birds sing, the mountains grow dark—

This is the wondrous power of Buddhism.
Ryokan, "Dewdrops on a Lotus Leaf"

The universe used to be seen as a majestic clockwork set of concentric spheres. Ptolemy developed a mathematical model with the earth at the centre that could be used to predict the motion of the stars and planets in the skies. Christian theologians used the science of their day to paint a picture of the universe as created by God (the uncreated source of all existence). Medieval thinkers placed this model within the context of the larger picture of existence that they had, namely the spiritual reality that envelopes this material world. They developed a picture of the universe surrounded by the prime mover, which was the force that propelled the planets.

The author of Sirach posits a God who wills the world to operate the way it does:

> By the word of the Lord his works are made;
> and all his creatures do his will.
> The sun looks down on everything with its light,
> and the work of the Lord is full of his glory.
>
> (Sirach 42: 15-16)

Norman Wirzba says: "the doctrine of creation reveals a divine intention. The universe is not simply a brute mass that has been left to its own devices, but serves a divine aim. And we, said to be created in the divine image, are called upon to bear witness to and emulate the creator's intention."[369] This will, however, is not fully known through his creation. In the wisdom literature of the Torah, the creation is spoken of as a highly ordered, even calculated act. The author of Sirach proceeds from observation of the creation muted by acknowledgement that we cannot know the depth of the richness of the true nature of things:

> The Lord has not empowered even his holy ones

---

[369] Norman Wirzba, *The Paradise of God: Renewing Religion in an Ecological Age* (Oxford, 2003), 13.

> to recount all his marvellous works,
>> which the Lord the Almighty has established
>>> so that the universe may stand firm in his glory.
>> (Sirach 42: 17)

Similarly, science displays a universe that astounds our imagination. There are about 80 billion stars visible with our modern telescopes, and we can't even observe the whole universe. In a universe so mind-bogglingly vast, our existence seems rather inconsequential.

In Sirach, the purpose of the universe is to display God's glory, a power that is beyond even human imagination. The wisdom of God reaches beyond human comprehension, and the universe itself displays this mystery to the human eye.

> For the Most High knows all that may be known;
>> he sees from of old the things that are to come.
> He discloses what has been and what is to be,
>> and he reveals the traces of hidden things.
> No thought escapes him,
>> and nothing is hidden from him.
> (Sirach 42: 18b-20)

God doesn't even know everything (only things that can logically be known) but the universe displays the constancy of God's wisdom.

The search for God's greatness displayed in nature never ends. It gives stimulus to the mind, since it seeks to understand the wisdom of the created order (not extrapolate the divine nature from that order, but understand how things work, so that we might understand the will of Him who made them).

> Many things greater than these lie hidden,
>> for I have seen but few of his works.
> For the Lord has made all things,
>> and to the godly he has given wisdom.
> (Sirach 43:32-33)

The laws of nature stay the same, although their manifold complexity is never fully revealed to us.

Creation as a sign

The world is charged with the grandeur of God.
It will flame out, like shining from shook foil;
It gathers to a greatness, like the ooze of oil
Crushed.
Gerard Manley Hopkins, "God's Grandeur"

Earth, air, fire and water used to be considered the basic elements of the universe. Aristotle theorized that the heavens must be of a different material (the quintessence), since they move in such perfectly predictable ways (according to the pristine laws of mathematics). Science has now given us a different picture of the fundamental basis of our material existence. Our model of nature continues to change as scientists discover smaller and smaller elementary particles. The more we dig down into the lowest levels of physical reality, the more we realize the complexity of the universe. Life seems to emerge from the structure of matter as it combines in unexpected ways. Even the mind is now thought of as produced somehow by the interactions within the physical brain.

Theology and science, however, have different insights based on their particular methods. Lee Smolin, in arguing for a purely scientific approach to reality, says:

> The possibility that the tremendous beauty of the living world might be, in the end, just a matter of randomness, statistics and frozen accident stands as a genuine threat to the mystical conceit that reality can be captured in a single, beautiful equation.[370]

---

[370] Lee Smolin, *The Life of the Universe* (Oxford, 1997), 180.

The scientific imagination achieves a vision of creation (that is, all things created) as a system of theoretical concepts. Religion, by contrast, has a more poetic vision of creation connected to a creative force. This creativity is mirrored in the human ability to create.

Theistic religions use the metaphor of mind to posit a supernatural mind. Philip Clayton argues that the idea of God acts as a regulative ideal:

> [R]eason is constrained to postulate a highest ideal, the ideal of the completion of reason or, in other cases, its highest instance. We are driven to conceive this highest ideal not merely as an epistemic principle but as a single instance. Only one being would, if it existed, represent this ideal consummation of reason: ... the most real being, or God.[371]

Does this idea refer to a real entity, or is it an illusion fostered by an overactive mind? Some would say that if science can provide an explanation for reality then the idea of God becomes superfluous. Where, then, does the rationality of the universe come from?

In a way, science is today being used to provide answers to longstanding religious questions. E. O. Wilson, one of the current champions of a complete scientific explanation of our reality, concedes:

> As science proceeds to dismantle the ancient mythic stories one by one, theology retreats to the final redoubt from which it can never be driven. This is the idea of God in the creative myth: God as will, the cause of existence, and the agent who generated all of the energy in the original fireball and set the natural laws by which the universe evolved. So long as the redoubt exists,

---

[371] Philip Clayton, "'Creative Mutual Interaction' as Manifesto, Research Program, and Regulative Ideal" in Ted Peters and Nathan Hallanger, eds. *God's Action in Nature's World* (Ashgate, 2006), 59.

theology can slip out through its portals and make occasional sallies back into the real world.[372]

He argues for an evolutionary epic as the prime myth for our modern age, since his naturalism precludes any recourse to divine agents as causes for the phenomena we encounter.

I propose, then, that we see the creation as a sign that, when read correctly, gives us some vision of the goodness of God. Arthur Peacocke summarizes a similar view:

> The created world is seen then by Christians as a symbol because it is a mode of God's revelation, an expression of his truth and beauty, which are the spiritual aspects of his reality. It is also valued by them for what God is effecting instrumentally through it: what God does in and through it.[373]

Like the Christian sacraments, which are both a visible sign of invisible grace and also a means of that grace (a way in which grace is mediated to people), creation can be seen as both pointing to God as well as being the matrix of God's nature expressed in material form. However, the signs are blurred by the reality that creation is fallen, and so does not always display the goodness of God.

God the creator has traditionally been understood as distinct from the creation. God's presence is displayed in nature (since it was created good). The Bible says that humans were created in the image of God. The actual structure of nature does not necessarily correspond to the being of God (so we cannot conclude that God is ordered or intelligible) but we can postulate that God is the kind of God that would want to create an ordered and intelligible universe. Further, the creation can be seen as a means of God's grace, since it was created good. Although fallen, creation displays some of the goodness that God intends

---

[372] E. O. Wilson, *On Human Nature* (Harvard University Press, 1978), 191.
[373] Arthur Peacocke, *The Palace of Glory: God's World and Science* (ATF Press, 2006), 82.

for us to experience. We must discern what aspects of nature contain God's intention and act so as to bring about their fruition.

Creation as icon

"What is the eye of the true Dharma? Everywhere."
Zen koan[374]

There are more things in heaven and earth, Horatio, than are dreamt of in your philosophy.
William Shakespeare, "Hamlet" Act 1 Scene V

Sometimes it seems like we have to translate from one language to another when we travel between the countries of science and faith. This cultural divide remains with us (evidenced in many of our universities). It is rare that students study both the classics of literature and the rigours of calculus. Even more, however, the churches are divorced from the educational institutions which they once helped to found. Schools of divinity are institutionally sidelined into academic irrelevance although their students are among the most broadly educated.

Of course, the church has contributed to the wall between science and faith, reacting defensively to each new intellectual challenge, retreating to the rocks of authority and tradition. Doubtlessly, there are times when faith must stubbornly resist to relinquish its judgment, but we should choose our intellectual battles wisely. Too often, faith is defended in a reactionary way, as if to believe something contrary to reason is a spiritual test. We should instead seek to understand science well enough to reason about our faith from within that outlook.

---

[374] John Daido Loori, *Sitting with Koans* (Simon and Schuster, 2012).

I propose that we see nature as an icon: a sign that points to the reality of God but in an indirect, artistic way. Vladimir Ouspensky defines an icon as "a powerful transmission, absolutely devoid of all emotional explanation, of a certain spiritual reality."[375] He is talking about the peculiar style of traditional Eastern Orthodox icons, which have a flat perspective in order to indicate that God's reality is different than ours. The popular conception is that icons represent God, but Ouspensky says: "The icon does not represent the divinity. Rather, it indicates man's participation in the divine life."[376] If we see nature as an icon, pointing to God, we must not simply read God's nature directly out of our nature. Instead, we must perform the same transformation that icon painters do when they paint a landscape or a human face. When we look at nature, we see it through our eyes, but we should filter it through the revelatory perspective of doctrine. Richard Fern sees God as a cosmic poet, "speaking the world into being" like a storyteller unfolding a tale according to its own inner logic. "[God] takes pleasure in and responds to the reflection of his eternal Self in the mirror of creation."[377] A theology of nature should put human nature in the foreground but also include a reading of the signs and symbols that are given to the human imagination through our study of the natural world around us.

Icons have traditionally been painted in a very stylized way, with human figures front and centre, but often with nature or the architecture of the region in the background. In the medieval period, this way of looking at nature was quite common. Ian Barbour argues that "[a]t times spiritual destiny seemed so to outweigh temporal relationships that the world was treated as a great allegory whose essential secret was its religious

---

[375] Vladimir Ouspensky, *Theology of the Icon* (St. Vladimir's Seminary Press, 1992), 166.
[376] Ibid.
[377] Richard Fern, *Nature, God and Humanity: Envisioning an Ethics of Nature* (Cambridge University Press, 2002), 146.

meaning, not its operation and its causes."[378] Nature was not taken seriously as a system in its own right although the 'book of nature' was seen as revealing something about God. The reality of this world paled in light of the next. As well, God's works in history overshadowed the acts of God's creative activity.

This survey of the issues confronting science and religion has compared the different metaphors that they use in the hope that some sustained reflection might move the debate forward in fruitful ways. In my view, theology can adapt scientific ideas like "energy" to speak about religious ideas. Jürgen Moltmann, for example, emphasizes the role of the Spirit in creation. He argues:

> It is always the Spirit who first brings the activity of the Father and the Son to its goal. It follows that the triune God also unremittingly breathes the Spirit into his creation. Everything that is, exists and lives in the unceasing inflow of the energies and potentialities of the cosmic Spirit. This means that we have to understand every created reality in terms of energy, grasping it as the realized potentiality of the divine Spirit. Through the energies and potentialities of the Spirit, the Creator is himself present in his creation.[379]

This would mean that creation is an outgrowth of the Trinitarian inter-relationships. Moltmann stresses that God's being does not require creation, but instead God's love in the relations between the persons of the Trinity flows outwards from God and is manifested in the creation, which is distinct from God's being, yet a product of it. Moltmann says: "In the free, overflowing rapture of his love the eternal God goes out of himself and makes a creation, a reality, which is there as he is there, and is yet

---

[378] Ian Barbour, *Religion and Science: Historical and Contemporary Issues* (HarperSanFrancisco: 1997), 6.
[379] Jürgen Moltmann, *God in Creation: A New theology of Creation and the Spirit of God* (SCM Press, 1985), 9.

different from himself."[380] Nature is not divine; it is other than God. In this God delights, allowing freedom to flourish, leaving the creation itself to bring the potentialities embedded within it to fruition (with good and bad consequences).

The way we talk about the world should echo the reality of God's work in this material reality. The Christian church has embraced a theology of presence not only in revelation but also in the cultural forms through which people express their faith. The icon, after some controversy, was accepted as a visual form that points to the reality of God in our midst. There is no way to indicate God's reality except by comparison with ours. Science is like the *Flatland* of Edwin Abbot, in which the creatures inhabiting a universe cannot envision more dimensions than the ones which they inhabit.[381] Today, theoretical physics is imaginative like theology since it envisions a world of many dimensions beyond that which we can see. However, it is still flat in the sense that it cannot see past the material.

Religions should aim to speak about those things that are beyond our vision. Paul says in I Corinthians 13:12: "We see through a glass, darkly." Theology should readily acknowledge its own limitations yet I think that it can still be a window through material reality (using matter to refract spirit). Science deliberately limits itself to that which can be sensed (and tries to represent reality in its theories). Theology takes the objects of our senses and tries to look through them, using them as icons of divine presence. Material things can be used to represent something of God's reality, but icons use codes and metaphors in order to speak indirectly. We can use science to talk about things beyond but we can only do so metaphorically.

If theology is truly "faith seeking understanding" (as Saint Anselm said) then it must take into account the current

---

[380] Ibid., 15.
[381] Edwin Abbott, *Flatland: A Romance of Many Dimensions* http://www.ibiblio.org/eldritch/eaa/FL.HTM

understandings of reality. Using all scientific resources, including neurological studies of the brain during religious experience, we should continue to ask: what is God doing in people's lives? This study would also require all of the resources of political science as well as sociology. Theology should start with the best scientific theories, asking what the traditional doctrines have to say given our best accounts of the world in which we live. Placing these in the context of the God "in whom we live and move and have our being" (Acts 17:28) would be a monumental task, requiring the cooperation of scientists and theologians. This dialogue should not result in turf wars but instead a probing, self-critical dialogue.

Bibliography

Abbott, Edwin. *Flatland: A Romance of Many Dimensions.* http://www.ibiblio.org/eldritch/eaa/FL.HTM

Aczel, Amir. *Why Science does not Disprove God.* William Morrow Publishers, New York: 2015.

Atran, Scott. *In Gods We Trust: The Evolutionary Landscape of Religion.* Oxford University Press, 2002.

Augustine. "The Literal Meaning of Genesis," trans. John Hammond Taylor, S. J. *Ancient Christian Writers* 41. Newman Press, 1982.

Bacon, Francis. *The New Organon and Related Writings*, ed. by Fulton Anderson. New York: Liberal Arts Press, 1960.

Barbour, Ian. *Myths, Models and Paradigms: A Comparative Study in Science and Religion.* Harper and Row, 1974.

Barbour, Ian. *Religion and Science: Historical and Contemporary Issues.* HarperSanFrancisco: 1997.

Barbour, Ian. *When Science Meets Religion.* HarperSanFrancisco: 2000.

Barrett, Justin. *Why Would Anyone Believe in God?* AltaMira Press, 2004.

Berry, Thomas and Brian Swimme. *The Universe Story: From the Primordial Flaring Forth to the Ecozoic Era—A Celebration of the Unfolding of the Cosmos.* HarperSanFrancisco, 1992.

Berry, Wendell. *Home Economics.* North Point Press, 1987.

Bonhoeffer, Dietrich. *Creation and Fall; Temptation.* London: SCM Press, 1959.

Boniolo, Giovanni and Gabriela de Ana, eds. *Evolutionary Ethics and Contemporary Biology.* Cambridge University Press, 2006.

Boyer, Pascal. *Religion Explained: The Evolutionary Origins of Religious Thought.* Basic Books, 2001.

Bronowski, Jacob. *The Origins of Knowledge and Imagination.* New Haven: Yale University Press, 1978.

Brooke, John Hedley. *Science and Religion: Some Historical Perspectives.* Cambridge University Press, 1991.

Broom, Harold M. *The Evolution of Morality and Religion.* Cambridge University Press, 2003.

Browning, Don and Terry Cooper. *Religious Thought and the Modern Psychologies.* Fortress Press, 2004.

Bruteau, Beatrice. *God's Ecstasy: The Creation of a Self-creating World.* Crossroad Pub. Co., 1997.

Bucaille, Maurice. *The Bible, the Qur'an and science: the Holy Scriptures examined in the light of modern knowledge.* Elmhurst, N.Y.: Tahrike Tarsile Quràn, 2003.

Burge, Ted. "A Creation Story for our Times," in Russell Stannard, *God for the 21st Century.* Templeton Foundation Press, 2000.

Campolo, Tony. *How to Rescue the Earth without Worshipping Nature.* T. Nelson Publishers, 1992.

Clark, Andy. *Being There: Putting Brain, Body and World Together Again.* MIT Press, 1997.

Clark, Andy. *Mindware: An Introduction to the Philosophy of Cognitive Science.* Oxford University Press, 2001.

Clayton, Philip. *Mind and Emergence: From Quantum to Consciousness.* Oxford, 2004.

Clayton, Philip. *Religion and Science: The Basics.* Routledge, 2013.

Clayton, Philip and Arthur Peacocke, eds. *In Whom We Live and Have our Being: Panentheistic Reflections on God's Presence in a Scientific World.* Eerdman's, 2004.

Clayton, Philip and Paul Davies, eds. *The Re-emergence of Emergence: The Emergentist Hypothesis from Science to Religion.* Oxford University Press, 2006.

Clayton, Philip and Jeffrey Schloss, eds. *Evolution and Ethics: Human Morality in Biological and Religious Perspectives.* Eerdman's. 2004.

Clayton, Philip and Zachary Simpson, eds. *The Oxford Handbook of Religion and Science.* Oxford, 2006.

Coleman, Richard. *State of Affairs*: *The Science-Theology Controversy.* Lutterworth Press, 2015.

Corey, Michael A. *Evolution and the Problem of Natural Evil.* University Press of America, 2000.

Coyne, George. *Faith and Knowledge: Towards a New Meeting of Science and Theology.* Libreria Editrice Vaticana, 2007.

Crick, Francis. *The Astonishing Hypothesis: The Scientific Search for the Soul.* Scribner, 1994.

D'Aquili, Eugene and Andrew Newberg. *Why God Won't Go Away: Brain Science and the Biology of Belief.* Ballantine Books, 2001.

Dalai Lama IV (Tenzin Gyatso). *The Universe in a Single Atom: The Convergence of Science and Spirituality.* New York: Morgan Road Books, 2005.

Damasio, Antonio. *The Feeling of What Happens: Body and Emotion in the Making of Consciousness.* Harcourt Brace, 1999.

Davies, Douglas James. *Anthropology and Theology.* Berg, 2002.

Davies, Paul. *God and the New Physics.* Simon and Schuster, 1983.

Davies, Paul. *The Mind of God.* Simon and Schuster, 1992.

Davies, Paul. *Superforce: The Search for a Grand Unified Theory of Nature.* Heinemann, 1984.

Dawkins, Richard. *The Blind Watchmaker.* Penguin, 1991.

Dawkins, Richard. *The God Delusion.* Houghton Mifflin, 2006.

Dawkins, Richard. *The Selfish Gene.* Oxford University Press, 1976.

De Waal, Frans. *Good Natured: The Origins of Right and Wrong in Humans and Other Animals.* Harvard University Press, 1996.

De Waal, Frans. *Primates and Philosophers: How Morality Evolved.* Princeton University Press, 2006.

Deane-Drummond, Celia. *Creation Through Wisdom: Theology and the New Biology.* T & T Clark, 2000.

Dembski, William. "Science and Design," *First Things* (October 1, 1998).

Dennett, Daniel. *Breaking the Spell: Religion as a Natural Phenomenon.* Penguin, 2006.

Denton, Michael. *Nature's Destiny: How the Laws of Biology Reveal Purpose in the Universe*. Free Press, 1998.

Dillard, Annie. *Pilgrim at Tinker Creek*. Bantam Books, 1975.

Dillenberger, John. *Protestant Thought and Natural Science*. Abingdon Press, 1960.

Domning, Daryl and Monika Hellwig. *Original Selfishness: Original Sin and Evil in the Light of Evolution*. Ashgate, 2006.

Edis, Taner. *An Illusion of Harmony: Science and Religion in Islam*. Prometheus Books, 2007.

Eliade, Mircea. *The Sacred and the Profane: The Nature of Religion*. Harper and Row, 1961.

Faw, Harold. *Psychology in Christian Perspective*. Baker Books, 1995.

Fehige, Yiftach, ed. *Science and Religion: East and West*. Routledge: 2016.

Ferris, Timothy, ed. *The World Treasury of Physics, Astronomy and Mathematics*. Little, Brown, 1981.

Fern, Richard. *Nature, God and Humanity: Envisioning an Ethics of Nature*. Cambridge University Press, 2002.

Ferngren, Gary. *Science and Religion: A Historical Introduction*. Johns Hopkins University Press, 2002.

Flew, Antony. *Evolutionary Ethics*. Macmillan, 1967.

Frank, Adam. *The Constant Fire: Beyond the Science vs. Religion Debate*. University of California Press, 2009.

Frye, Northrop. *The Double Vision: Language and Meaning in Religion.* University of Toronto Press, 1991.

Galilei, Galileo. "Letter to the Grand Duchess Christina" http://www.fordham.edu/halsall/mod/galileo-tuscany.html

Giberson, Karl and Francis Collins. *The Language of Science and Faith.* InterVarsity Press, 2011.

Gladwell, Malcolm. *Blink: The Power of Thinking without Thinking.* Little, Brown and Co., 2005.

Goodenough, Ursula. *The Sacred Depths of Nature.* Oxford University Press, 1998.

Goodenough, Ursula. *The Sacred Foundations of Nature.* Oxford University Press, 1998.

Gould, Stephen Jay. *Rocks of Ages: Science and Religion in the Fullness of Life.* Ballantine Pub. Group, 1999.

Gregorios, Metropolitan Paulos Mar. "A Theory of Nature: An Introduction." http://www.goarch.org/ourfaith/ourfaith8045

Gribbin, John. *Unveiling the Edge of Time.* Crown Publishers, 1992.

Haag, James W. Gregory Peterson and Michael Spezio, eds. *Routledge Companion to Religion and Science.* Routledge, 2012.

Hauser, Mark. *Moral Minds: How Nature Designed our Universal Sense of Right and Wrong.* Ecco, 2006.

Haught, John. *Science and Religion: From Conflict to Conversation.* Paulist Press, 1995.

Hawking, Stephen W. *A Brief History of Time: From the Big Bang to Black Holes.* Bantam Books, 1988.

Hawking, Stephen. *Stephen Hawking's* A Brief History of Time*: A Reader's Companion.* Bantam Books, 1992.

Hawking, Stephen. *The Universe in a Nutshell.* Bantam Spectra, 2001.

Heisenberg, Werner. *Physics and Philosophy.* Prometheus Books, 1999.

Henig, Robin Marantz. "Darwin's God." *New York Times Magazine*, March 4, 2007.

Hick, John. *The New Frontier of Religion and Science: Religious Experience, Neuroscience and the Transcendent.* Palgrave Macmillan, 2006.

Hitt, Jack. "This is Your Brain on God" *Wired* 7.11 Nov. 1999 http://www.wired.com/wired/archive/7.11/persinger.html

Hodge, Charles. *Systematic Theology.* New York: Scribners, 1872.

Hodgson, Peter. *Science and Belief in the Nuclear Age.* Sapientia Press of Ave Maria University, 2006.

Hodgson, Peter. *Theology and Modern Physics.* Ashgate, 2005.

Honner, John. "Cosmology and the Creed" *Compass* 14 (Sept./Oct. 1993).

Hooykas, Reijer. *Religion and the Rise of Modern Science.* Grand Rapids: Eerdman's, 1972.

Huchingson, James. *Pandemonium Tremendum: Chaos and Mystery in the Life of God.* Pilgrim Press, 2001.

Huxley, T. H. *Evolution and Ethics.* Appleton, 1929.

Ingram, Paul. *Buddhist-Christian dialogue in an age of science.* Rowman and Littlefield, 2008.

James, William. *The Varieties of Religious Experience.* Harvard University Press, 1985.

Jeeves, Malcolm and R. J. Berry, *Science, Life and Christian Belief.* Apollos, 1998.

John Paul II, "Address, Jubilee of Scientists." (May 25, 2000). http://www.cin.org/pope/jubilee-scientists.html

Joyce, Richard. *The Evolution of Morality.* MIT Press, 2006.

Kaku, Michio and Jennifer Thompson. *Beyond Einstein.* Anchor Books, 1995.

Kaufman, Gordon D. "A Religious Interpretation of Emergence: Creativity as God." *Zygon: Journal of Religion & Science.* December 1, 2007.

Kellert, Stephen R. and Timothy J. Farnham, eds. *The Good in Nature and Humanity: Connecting Science, Religion and Spirituality with the Natural World.* Washington, D.C.: Island Press, 2002.

Klaaren, Eugene. *Religious Origins of Modern Science.* Grand Rapids: Eerdman's, 1977.

Kuhn, Thomas. *The Structure of Scientific Revolutions.* University of Chicago Press, 1970.

Küng, Hans and David Tracy, eds. *Paradigm Change in Theology: A Symposium for the Future.* Edinburgh: T & T Clark, 1989.

Langford, Jerome. *Galileo, Science and the Church,* Third Edition. Ann Arbor: University of Michigan Press, 1992.

Larson, E. J. and L. Witham. "Scientists Are Still Keeping the Faith." *Nature* 386 (3 April 1997). http://www.nature.com/nature/journal/v386/n6624/pdf/386435a0.pdf

Larson, E. J. and L. Witham. "Leading Scientists Still Reject God." *Nature* 395 (1998). http://www.stephenjaygould.org/ctrl/news/file002.html

Ledger, Christine and Stephen Pickard, eds. *Creation and Complexity: Interdisciplinary Issues in Science and Religion.* Adelaide: ATF Press, 2004.

Lindberg, David and Ronald Numbers, eds. *God and Nature.* University of California Press, 1986.

Lodge, David and Christopher Hamlin, eds. *Religion and the New Ecology: Environmental Responsibility in a World of Flux.* University of Notre Dame Press, 2006.

Lovelock, James. *The Ages of Gaia: A Biography of our Living Earth.* Norton, 1988.

Lewis, C. S. *The Four Loves.* Harcourt, Brace, 1960.

Maienschein, Jane and Michael Ruse, eds., *Biology and the Foundation of Ethics.* Cambridge; New York: Cambridge University Press, 1999.

McGrath, Alister. *The Foundations of Dialogue in Science and Religion.* Blackwell, 1998.

McGrath, Alister. *The Order of Things: Explorations in Scientific Theology.* Blackwell, 2006.

McGrath, Alister. "Science and the Social Order." *Philosophy of Science* 5, 321-337, 1938

McGrath, Alister. *A Scientific Theology* Vol 1: *Nature*; Vol. 2: *Reality*; Vol. 3; *Theory*. London: Continuum and Grand Rapids, MI: Eerdman's, 2003.

McMinn, Mark R. *Care for the Soul: Exploring the Intersection of Psychology & Theology*. InterVarsity Press, 2001.

McNamara, Patrick, ed. *Where God and Science Meet*. V.1 Praeger Publishers, 2006.

Murphy, Nancey. *Theology in the Age of Scientific Reasoning*. Cornell University Press, 1990.

Nebelsick, Harold P. *The Renaissance, the Reformation and the Rise of Science*. Edinburgh: T&T Clark, 1992.

Newton, Isaac. "General Scholium" from *Principia Mathematica*. https://isaac-newton.org/general-scholium/

Merton, Robert. *Science, Technology and Society in Seventeenth Century England*. OSIRIS: Studies on the History and Philosophy of Science and on the History of Learning and Culture. Bruges, Belgium: St. Catherine Press, 1938.

Midgley, Mary. *Beast and Man: The Roots of Human Nature*. Methuen, 1980.

Miller, Kenneth R. *Finding Darwin's God*. Cliff Street Books, 1999.

Miller, Keith, ed. *Perspectives on an Evolving Creation*. Eerdman's, 2003.

Moltmann, Jürgen. *God in Creation: A New Theology of Creation and the Spirit of God*. SCM Press, 1985.

Moltmann, Jurgen. *Science and Wisdom*. SCM Press, 2003.

Murphy, Nancey. *Bodies and Souls, or Spirited Bodies?* Cambridge University Press, 2006.

Murphy, Nancey and George Ellis. *On the Moral Nature of the Universe: Theology, Cosmology and Ethics.* Fortress, 1996.

Murphy, Nancey and William Stoeger, *Evolution and Emergence: Systems, Organisms, Persons.* Oxford University Press, 2007.

Myers, David and Malcolm Jeeves. *Psychology Through the Eyes of Faith.* Christian College Coalition, 1987.

Neff, David. "The Pope, the Press and Evolution," *Christianity Today* (January 6, 1997).

Nitecki, Matthew H. and Doris V. Nitecki, eds. *Evolutionary Ethics.* Albany, NY: State University of New York Press, 1993.

Noring, Jon. "A Summary of Personality Testing." http://www.wiredbrain.net//types.htm

Nygren, Anders. *Agape and Eros.* SPCK, 1982.

O'Murchu, Diarmuid. *Evolutionary Faith.* Orbis Books, 2002.

O'Murchu, Diarmuid. *Quantum Theology.* Crossroad, 1997.

Olson, Richard. *Science and Religion 1450-1900: From Copernicus to Darwin.* Greenwood Press, 2004.

Ouspensky, Vladimir. *Theology of the Icon.* St. Vladimir's Seminary Press, 1992.

Pannenberg, Wolfhart. *Toward a Theology Nature: Essays on Science and Faith.* Westminster/J. Knox Press, 1993.

Pascal, Blaise. *Pensées.* Penguin Books, 1966.

Peacocke, Arthur. *The Palace of Glory: God's World and Science.* ATF Press, 2006.

Peacocke, Arthur. *Paths From Science Towards God: The End of all Our Exploring.* Oneworld, 2001.

Penrose, Roger. *Shadows of the Mind: A Search for the Missing Science of Consciousness.* Oxford University Press, 1994.

Peters, Ted and Nathan Hallanger, eds. *God's Action in Nature's World: Essays in Honour of Robert John Russell.* Ashgate, 2006.

Peters, Ted and Gaymon Bennett, eds. *Bridging Science and Religion.* Fortress, 2003.

Pinker, Steven. *How the Mind Works.* W. W. Norton, 1997.

Polanyi, Michael. *Science, Faith and Society.* University of Chicago Press, 1964.

Polkinghorne, John. *Quantum Theory: A Very Short Introduction.* Oxford University Press, 2002.

Polkinghorne, John. *Quarks, Chaos and Christianity.* Crossroad, 1996.

Pope John Paul II, "Magisterium is Concerned with Question of Evolution for it Involves Conception of Man." http://www.cin.org/jp2evolu.html

Popper, Karl. *The Logic of Scientific Discovery.* London: Hutchison, 1972.

Rambachan, Anantanand. *A Hindu theology of liberation: Not-two is not one.* Albany, NY: SUNY Press, 2015.

Ratzsch, Del. *Philosophy of Science: The Natural Sciences in Christian Perspective*. InterVarsity Press, 1986.

Ridley, Matt. *The Origins of Virtue*. Viking, 1996.

Roberts, Robert C. and Mark R. Talbot, eds. *Limning the Psyche*. Grand Rapids, MI: W.B. Eerdmans, 1997.

Rolston, Holmes, ed. *Biology, Ethics, and the Origins of Life*. Boston: Jones and Bartlett, 1995.

Russell, Robert John et al, eds. *Physics, Philosophy and Theology*. Vatican Observatory Foundation, 1988.

Russell, Robert, Nancey Murphy, Theo Meyering, Michael Arbib, eds. *Neuroscience and the Person: Scientific Perspectives on Divine Action*. Vatican Observatory, 1999.

Sacks, Oliver. *The Man Who Mistook his Wife for a Hat*. London: Duckworth, 1985.

Saunders, Nicholas. *Divine Action and Modern Science*. Cambridge University Press, 2002.

Schleiermacher, Friedrich. *On Religion: Speeches to its Cultured Despisers*. Cambridge University Press, 1988.

Shermer, Michael. *The Science of Good and Evil*. Times Books, 2004.

Shinn, Roger, ed. *Faith and Science in an Unjust World* Vol. 1. Fortress Press, 1980.

Smolin, Lee. *The Life of the Universe*. Oxford, 1997.

Southgate, Christopher, *et al*. *God, Humanity and the Cosmos*. 2nd edition. T & T Clark, 2005.

Snow, C. P. *The Two Cultures.* London; New York: Cambridge University Press, 1993.

Soskice, Janet Martin. *Metaphor and Religious Language.* Clarendon Press, 1987.

Stannard, Russell. *God for the 21st Century.* Templeton Foundation Press, 2000.

Stannard, Russell. "The Prayer Experiment: Does Prayer Work?" *Second Opinion* 2. (January 2000)

Stump, J. B. and Alan Padgett, eds. *The Blackwell Companion to Science and Christianity.* (Wiley-Blackwell). 2012

Sweet, William and Richard Feist, eds. *Religion and the Challenges of Science.* Ashgate, 2007.

Swimme, Brian. *The Universe is a Green Dragon : A Cosmic Creation Story.* Santa Fe, N.M.: Bear, 1985.

Tillich, Paul. *The Spiritual Situation in our Technical Society.* Macon, GA: Mercer University Press, 1988.

Van Huyssteen, Wentzel. *Alone in the World? Human Uniqueness in Science and Theology.* Eerdman's, 2006.

Van Huyssteen, Wentzel. *Duet or Duel? Theology and Science in a Postmodern World.* Trinity Press, 1998.

Vitz, Paul. *Psychology as Religion: The Cult of Self-worship.* W.B. Eerdmans, 1994.

Ward, Keith. *God, Chance and Necessity.* Oneworld, 1996.

Watts, Fraser, ed. *Science Meets Faith.* SPCK, 1998.

Watts, Fraser. *Theology and Psychology.* Ashgate, 2002.

White, Jr. Lynn. *Machina ex Deo: Essays in the Dynamism of Western Culture*. Cambridge, MA: Massachusetts Institute of Technology Press, 1968.

Whitehead, Alfred North. *Science and the Modern World.* Macmillan, 1962.

Whitehouse, Harvey and James Laidlaw, *Religion, Anthropology and Cognitive Science.* Carolina Academic Press, 2007.

Witham, Larry. *Where Darwin Meets the Bible*. Oxford University Press, 2002.

Wilson, E. O. *On Human Nature*. Harvard University Press, 1978.

Wirzba, Norman. *The Paradise of God: Renewing Religion in an Ecological Age.* Oxford, 2003.

Wright, Robert. *The Moral Animal: Evolutionary Psychology and Everyday Life.* Pantheon Books, 1994.

Young, Matt and Taner Edis, eds. *Why Intelligent Design Fails.* Rutgers University Press, 2004.

Zizioulas, John. *Being as Communion*. St. Vladimir's Seminary Press, 1985.

www.ingramcontent.com/pod-product-compliance
Lightning Source LLC
LaVergne TN
LVHW051519070426
835507LV00023B/3192